DON'T HASSLE ME,
I'M LOCAL

Vaughn

DON'T HASSLE ME, I'M LOCAL

The Travelogue of a Journey to Another Dimension

WINDYRIDGE

DON'T HASSLE ME, I'M LOCAL
A WINDYRIDGE BOOK

First published in Great Britain 2005 by Windyridge,
Selside, Kendal, Cumbria.

Copyright © Vaughn 2005

2nd Edition 2006
ISBN 0-9550434-1-7

Printed and bound by
Arti Grafiche Srl.,
Rome, Italy.

Until one is committed, there is always the chance to draw back; always ineffectiveness. Concerning all acts of initiative and creation there is one elementary truth, the ignorance of which kills countless ideas and splendid plans, that truth being that the moment one definitely commits oneself, then providence moves too. All sorts of things occur to help one that would not have otherwise occurred. A whole stream of events issue from the decision, raising in one's favour all manner of unforeseen incidents and meetings and material assistance which no man could have dreamt would come his way.

Whatever you can do or dream you can do, begin it. Boldness has genius, magic and power. Begin it now.

Goethe

For Cristina.
Her patience, love and understanding brought this book
to life.

● ☼♀♂ ☺ ♥♠@Ψ♫

CONTENTS

Some names and places have been changed to protect the identity of those concerned.

INTRODUCTION

Along a 5-mile stretch of the North Norfolk coast, desi-
gnated by the district council as an area of outstanding
natural beauty, lie the villages of Salthouse, Cley,
Wiveton, Blakeney and Morston.

One hundred years ago the vast majority of the families which
formed these communities, had been here for many generations. Imagine living in a place where everyone knows everything about everyone, going way back into the past; such shared understanding within a community must have given its
members an immense sense of harmony and security.

The amount of labour needed in the ports and farming had
been declining steadily for many years. By the 1960s
things were looking pretty bleak for this deep-rooted community. Televisions in every home painted magical dreams of exciting places beyond the world they knew, luring
many of the younger generations into deserting what they
perceived to be the sinking ship. With the children gone it
was only a matter of time before wealthy incomers snapped up the supply of surplus housing. This influx started a
rise in property prices, which created a problem for those
younger generations that were committed to staying. The
saddest part of it all was that, paradoxically, the incomers
who were falling over themselves to buy into the peace
and harmony of the old community were, in essence,
destroying that which they sought to possess.

1

Two very different communities now exist; the first being the deep-rooted remnants of the few old families who manage to stay; they, as we did, found a way into tourism, the only industry that remains in the area. The second is formed by those incomers who, finding it hard to integrate, form an alternative community that exists only on the surface; greatly outnumbering the old families. It is this veneer that is usually seen.

The families who remain do so as islands amidst a swirl of these transient incomers who arrive with all good intentions to stay but tomorrow are gone. This makes it a sad place to live. Sad because I glimpsed how it was long ago. To have had that privilege becomes a curse as I watch the disintegration of that "old way of life" as it becomes quietly overwhelmed.

And I sell holidays in this place. I tell our guests of its beauty and pretend that the new community of incomers can replace that of the old. I tell how they are our saviours because their arrival heralded the birth of the new industry of tourism but, alas, in truth the substance has been replaced by a shadow.

A commodity broker from the city whose dealings have made him a fortune buys a large house in the village. We have no idea who he is or what he has done to get his big house. He can tell us who he is and what he has done to get his big house, but why should we believe him; some folk plead "You must judge a tree by its fruits and not its roots", but how can we know the fruits of this man before he arrived in our land? We give him a chance and wait for him to reveal who he is within the community, but that requires a great amount of effort on the incomer's part. In fact, it requires a complete change of lifestyle because the only community he knows is the fast moving, city, hard, business, buying and selling, making money community which he came from. He decides it's easier and more comfortable to associate with all the other incomers who also found it hard to integrate. Instead they form a community of their own. Initially they take up a cause, they hold charity fundraisers for the restoration of the church, and they can be whoever they want, because the things they did to become who they really are took place a million miles from our sleepy little backwater. Their new friends don't ask too many questions or dig too deep, so they don't in return.

So here I stand, an island amidst a swirling sea of visitors, all drawn by the outstanding natural beauty of the place I know as home.

Sometimes I feel like a character in one of those speeded up videos; the one who remains still, perhaps leaning against a lamp-post, while the crowds of the streets come and go. And the faster they come and go, the less they register until they disappear completely.

My island can be a lonely place but it has its advantages. Island life allows time for contemplation of what some might regard the deeper issues. This story is my attempt at making sense of those issues. It describes the simple thoughts of a simple man that gave birth to a simple theory concerning the unifying field that connects all things throughout the universe.

In order to test the theory it was placed before Stephen Hawking, whose response was indeed positive. (When you live in a universe where all things are connected then all things are possible.)

The theory looks far beyond the mud flats and coastal villages of North Norfolk to provide a material, scientific interpretation of the universe that will take you, quite literally, out of this world.

From the solitude of the saltmarshes and shingle beaches came a realisation that it was the removal of this material, scientific explanation from the teachings of all the major world religions that has bestowed upon their leaders their esoteric power.

To suppose such a premeditated corruption had taken place would require that my theory had existed before the religion that corrupted it, in which case the theory isn't mine after all – I just re-discovered it – as have many others.

Just as a genealogist traces a bloodline, I began to trace a line of philosophy which took me back three thousand years. From the present day the line passed through the birth of Christ and his education by the Magi through Greek and Roman poets and philosophers and on into antiquity.

This is my story; a true local who has spent half a lifetime contemplating the deeper issues that touch us all. It's about a raw struggle for survival and the simplicity that I found in a society which seeks to complicate and confuse.

Don't Hassle Me, I'm Local

I was born on Grandmother's settee at 9 p.m. on the 7th of September 1956 in a house that is at the lowest point in Wiveton, a small village a mile from the North Norfolk coast.

Being a mile inland couldn't protect the cottage from the sea, witness 1953, when the area was flooded to such an extent that the previous occupier, a Mrs Dix, was drowned in her living room. This happened on the evening of the very day my grandfather bought the property, called "The Willows", which consisted of a pair of semi-detached farm-worker's cottages and a derelict barn. Mrs Dix was the sitting tenant whose untimely demise made way for my parents to move into the cottage.

A greater twist of fate brought my parents together when mother's previous husband also met a horrific end. They lived in a cottage in Stiffkey, which is a couple of miles down the coast from Wiveton. He was a young pilot who in 1947 had just got his wings. Excited and full of brava-do he decided to "buzz" their house with his Spitfire. Misjudging his height he clipped the ridge of the barn opposite. Imagine the horror. He died in a ball of flames in their garden.

I grew up and worked locally in the building trade just as my father and grandfather and great grandfather etc (the family has been in the area for a long while) and in 1985

☺

met Cristina, then a sister at the local hospital. We formed a partnership that conceived and brought into this world not only two children but also many twists of fate, luck and good fortune.

Some 20 years later we find ourselves making our living from three holiday cottages in the grounds of our house, *Broadview,* all of which were built by us, in the village where I was born.

When I say we built the properties that is literally what I mean. Every flint we picked from the quarry; every brick and tile we laid. Using local materials and your own labour has to be the most eco-friendly, cheapest and rewarding method of construction.

We bought *Broadview* in the summer of 1988. Back then all that stood on the site was a dilapidated 1920s timber bungalow with an asbestos roof. When the vultures that did the house clearance for the previous owner, a Mr Dusgate, had finished ruthlessly going over their spoils, it had the appearance of a large shed that had been vandalised.

Mr Dusgate's wife had passed away a few years earlier and having no family or reason to stay at *Broadview,* he decided, at the age of 82, to sell up everything and go and live with a nephew in Costa Rica. Sitting in *Broadview's* then cosy lounge we cemented the deal with a cup of tea and a handshake. The old gentleman told us he intended to live out the rest of his days in the sun. Rubbing his chin he dreamt out loud: "I love bananas and out there they are ten a penny... I'll live like a king." He sat dreaming of sun and Central American beaches so long that it required a diplomatic cough from Cristina to bring him back to the present.

We would move in and have to "make do" until we decided how best to go about the development of *Broadview*. During this time I was drawn to a mirror hanging in an old ivy covered garden shed.

"A strange place to hang a mirror", I thought.

Removing it from its place among the cobwebs I found, pasted on its back, a colour picture of Jane Russell, a movie star, cut from a magazine dated 1947. Strange creatures us humans. We invest so much time in hiding ourselves.

After making the timber bungalow habitable, which took a couple of months, we applied for and received planning permission to build a brick and flint skin around it and to construct a completely independent roof structure that would cover the old. The master plan was that with the bungalow thus encased we would build a large extension across the east end, so that the floor plan of the structure resembled a massive "T". This completed, we would move into the extension and remove the old timber *Broadview* from within the new.

Such dreams are easily conjured up and just as easily turned to plans by drawing lines on paper, but when it comes to turning those plans and dreams into something more substantial – that's when the real work begins.

The flints which we build with, are abstracted from quarries in surrounding villages. If a quarry has a grading machine then all the aggregate is dug out of the ground and placed in a gigantic hopper that feeds a conveyor belt; this carries everything up and into the grading machine. From there it makes its way through large revolving drums that sieve the aggregate on to various belts and chutes which channel the separated spoil into bays ranging from fine sand to flints which are no more than five inches – that's 125 mm – in diameter. Washed and graded, these flints cost around £160 a ton. If, however, you go to a quarry which doesn't have a grading machine, then all such flints are heaped up awaiting removal to a crushing machine which will reduce them to fragments that, mixed with sharp sand, will become the base mix for concrete which is sold at £12 per ton.

One such quarry, without a grading machine, lets us pick flints off the pile destined for the crusher. It takes about an hour and a half to pick a ton, which they sell to us for the same price as the concrete mix. I hope this description of our money saving schemes gives you some idea of how tight our budget was! Of course, what isn't seen at the time is the physical cost which said schemes exert on one's body, much of which only becomes apparent years later with the premature onset of arthritis – but that's enough of such whingeing.

The grading machine at one of the more played out quarries is a wonder to behold. When in action its drums, conveyor belts and chutes take on a life of their own. Held together by pieces of wire and binder twine and constantly percolating in torrents of water, the rattling and clanking of this rusting monster echo around the crater that it has consumed out of the Norfolk landscape.

One summer's day I found myself standing before this spectacle with Mick, a guest to whom I was giving a guided tour of the quarries in the area.

A retired Yorkshire miner, with a recent heart by-pass, Mick used to be in charge of the machinery that propped up the tunnel at the coal face. His obvious interest in mining had prompted me to take him on this tour; another less obvious reason for me treating Mick to the excursion was an event that had occurred the previous day.

Mick is a keen birdwatcher so I had taken him over to the watch-house in our new boat *"Eos"*. Situated just off the shingle bar between Cley beach and Blakeney Point, the watch-house is indeed a remote place. Once a coastguard's lookout, it had been sold to the National Trust who leased it to Girl Guides Society in 1932. They used it for many years before Blakeney parish took up the lease. Blakeney parish undertook the structural repairs that the building so desperately needed, and then began renting it to the general public.

Our friends, Ray and Wendy, have rented it many times, usually over mid-summer's day, and although the building is now structurally sound, there is still no running water or electricity. The loo, which you have to flush with a pail, is outside and the internal décor, furniture, fixtures and fittings are done in that unmistakable squat style.

On Ray and Wendy's first stay at the watch-house we managed to entice Cristina over for the day by creating a romantic description of Laura Ashley and bare pine, but that's another story.

Despite its lack of material refinements a more peaceful and relaxing rental property would be difficult to find round here. At mid-summer the sun only just manages to dip itself into the sea before rising again a few degrees to the east, the darkness of the night sky never entirely smothering its glow. Although it's only a small step closer to living with Mother Earth, being there in the warm summer evenings with no other soul for miles in any direction brings your senses to life. Colours, sounds and smells become intense – strangely new. Cradled in such raw natural beauty, with the imposing lights of the up-market Blakeney Hotel twinkling in the estuary before you, it's hard not to reflect on the irony of the situation. Two radically different interpretations of beauty, power and freedom.

Ray and Wendy were staying at the watch-house, so we'd had a pot of tea and they'd proudly given Mick a guided tour. We'd watched the seals playing in the sea just over the shingle bank and the Burnet six-spot moths flashing their red and black wings looking for mates on the causeway. Catching the tide as it turned, we made our way back to our jetty at Cley Mill. Chatting to Mick about this and that I leaned over the stern to attach the mooring rope. I could feel the bow drifting out as it always does, and with the stern securely fastened, I straightened up and turned, in order to do the same at the other end.

Nothing could have prepared me for what I was about to see. Well, I say nothing, but something must have, because Mick was one of the very few guests I had specifically asked to wear a life jacket.

Mick is one of those people who always like to be involved; to help me moor the boat he had kept hold of the jetty but, unable to hold the bow in, was now stretched between the two forming a bridge like a character from a Bugs and Daffy cartoon.

I grabbed Mick around the waist but knew from the outset that the force of gravity was going to be the winner, and so, after a short struggle, Mick disappeared headfirst over the side. Fortunately, the life jacket brought him back to the surface like a cork. Seeing that he was OK and was holding on to the jetty, I quickly removed his camera and binoculars which hung around his neck tangled amongst garlands of seaweed, and then helped him up out of the murky water, praying that his heart by-pass would hold out.

Despite his camera and binoculars being ruined Mick took it well, conceding that it had been his fault. His wife showed no sign of alarm when I returned him to her drenched in creek water, foul-smelling mud and weeds. She treated it as a matter of fact that Mick was prone to such accidents. Perhaps we bonded during the episode. I like to think that despite his impromptu dip I would still have taken him on the tour of the quarries, which now found us standing before Glaven Pit's grading machine, but if the truth be known, at the back of my mind there was a certain element of sucking up going on, inspired by paranoia of our fearful American cousin ... litigation.

Back to the renovation of Broadview.

We built around the timber bungalow and then got the planning permission for the large extension, which we built with the intention of moving into it so that we might then remove the old timber bungalow, along with its antiquated plumbing, electricity and heating systems. Unfortunately, this removal of the old timber bungalow would be a long time coming.

Out of the blue, just as we were finishing the large extension, we were offered the opportunity of buying the pieces of land to the east and west of us – which we jumped at. The previous occupier of these pieces of land was an easy-going, likeable chap but he had allowed the properties to become what resembled landfill sites! They were supposedly used for storage of boats and caravans, but wrecked cars and rubbish surrounded mountains of rat-infested garden waste from his friend's landscaping business. In fact anything he, or his friends, didn't want in their gardens was dumped next to ours! What made matters worse, he was the chairman of the village Parish Council!

It eventually came to light that the chairman's aunt actually owned the land; she had allowed her nephew to use it as his own when she had moved to Scotland 20 years previously. The lady was an old friend of our family who, after making a long overdue and unscheduled visit to Wiveton, was unhappy with what she saw and offered the land to us.

So, as I mentioned, we jumped at the offer. Taking this land from the nephew is not a thing I am proud of. At the time I told myself, It's business and there is no room for sentiment in business, but it didn't sit easily with me then or now, and that's the real price we had to pay for the land. With that sincere apology out in the open, I'll continue with the story. We immediately applied for and obtained planning permission to build a large double garage and workshop on one of the sites. Before we had even started the work, the District Council, in a drive to promote tourism, changed their planning policy to allow any existing building in the countryside permission for change of use for holiday accommodation. This meant that all we had to do was build the garages and then we could change them into holiday accommodation.

This was even worse news for the chairman of the Parish Council, as some six months earlier, just before we bought the land from his aunt, the District Council had refused him permission to build a bungalow of similar proportions on the same site!

Understandably, when we applied for change of use, the Parish Council went against us, but we were working with the District Council, who were advising us what to do and how to get the permission. It was an awkward situation, but much to the parish councillor's consternation we got our planning permit. Only when the holiday accommodation was complete did we turn our attention to the main house.

It was 2001 when we finally moved into the extension in order to remove the timber bungalow. That renovation took a couple of years and, when it was done we cut the large extension in two, incorporating half of it into our new house, the other half becoming *Alice,* a one-bedroom holiday annexe.

The previously converted garages and workshop became *Hatter* and *March Hare.* They have been running from 1999 and 2001 respectively, and with *Alice* coming on line in the spring of 2003, we were finally making a living.

Letting out the holiday cottages we meet all sorts. Each has a story to tell. Some choose to hold their anonymity close, which we respect, others give colour and depth to our world as they share their experiences, hopes and dreams.

Two astronomers who come to stay marvel at our great expanses of crystal clear night sky. They are the proud owners of Galileo, their home-made 12″ reflector telescope. The construction of such an instrument requires a depth of understanding that completes the link between them and the distant galaxies they show us. I feel so small and insignificant as they take us to the craters of the moon or the planets of our solar system and beyond.

Until meeting them I had taken my countryside view of the Milky Way for granted, not realising how light pollution turns city skies into an orange soup.

Thousands of years ago our ancestors would not have had to contend with the pollution that intrudes into every aspect of life in the 21st century. Their lives were lived naturally, they knew their connection instinctively, they knew they were part of the bigger picture.

It's interesting work letting out the cottages. We like to meet people and they come to us from all walks of life. I'm not suggesting it's something we intend to do for the rest of our lives, but just at the moment the guests are good company. We meet healers, each with their individual gift, carers, teachers of every subject, firemen, policemen, doctors, nurses, artists working in every medium, farmers, miners, sail-makers, mechanics of cars, aeroplanes, helicopters and all manner of machines, information technology consultants, gamekeepers, fitness advisers – the list goes on and on. Every one of them is unique, but they all have one thing in common, they come to *Broadview* to escape the pollution, be it mental or environmental, that has become so pervasive these days.

Under the guise of birdwatching, walking, astronomy, whatever flips the switch, we each have our way of escaping – even if it's only for a little while.

PAINTING IN OILS

With the cottages finally earning us a living, the pressure was off, so I thought I'd try my hand at expressing my innermost feelings by painting in oils. A few years earlier and far too many years too late for such capers, some friends and I put together a 4-piece rock band. We called ourselves *"The Point"* and played original songs written by the lead guitarist and me. We poured out these sour songs to empty village halls and clubs all around this part of Norfolk. This form of expression required the co-operation of Johnny Picnic, the proprietor of our local deli, on drums; Mark Drake, a BMW paint sprayer, on bass, and Brian Eade, music teacher and owner of the PA, on lead guitar. At the time it was great fun, but looking back, I have to classify it amongst those embarrassing learning experiences that closed doors in order to facilitate a necessary change of direction.

One day I happened to be in the near-by market town of Holt, and on an impulse went into a gallery of paintings. I looked at them. Hmm. I could do that, I thought.

Rolf Harris poses the question, "Why is it that at the age of 4 when we enter the schooling system and are given some paints or crayons and a piece of paper, we can create a picture which reflects our feelings, yet 13 years later, when we leave that schooling system 98% of us are certain we have lost that ability?". It can only be down to the fact that as we grow into that said schooling system we

☻♠

become more self-conscious. Our teachers' and peers' perception of what constitutes the norm moulds and pigeonholes the individual, while in the process crushing creativity. Sadly, if you're told often enough that you can't do something, you can end up believing it yourself.

Of course there are exceptions to this rule. I remember my secondary school music teacher throwing up his hands while despairing to the class that I was tone deaf – yet still I persisted with *The Point.*

In September 2002 I bought some paints, brushes, canvasses, palettes and an easel from the free ads. A chap was giving it up for the trombone. It was a real bargain, £90 the lot. Just how much of a bargain I found out when, after realising my love for cobalt blue and liberally covering several canvases with one of the free ad tubes, I visited the art shop to replenish my supply and discovered that such beautiful colours are very expensive. Ever since I've used them with a little more respect, though never so much as would cramp my style.

Now some schools of thought say the meaning of a painting should be left for the viewer to discover for him- or her-self, others think it's interesting to know why the picture was painted. Well I've considered both views and decided on the latter.

PSYCHOLOGY
(Oil on canvas 20″ x 16″)

From the moment of our birth, maybe even conception, we begin to build a wall, from behind which we will view the world. That wall is made from all our life experiences, the paradox being that the experiences from which the wall is built dictate what we see through its window. For instance, through the window in a wall built from love, we might see a light open landscape inhabited by happy people where anything is possible, but on the other hand, a wall built from fear might have bars on the window and monsters looming in the darkness beyond.

Our walls are unique to each and every one of us, but as we come to understand their construction we realise the picture we see is just an illusion we have created, and from that point the wall and the illusion begin to fade.

We become as free as a butterfly.

RELIGION
(Oil on canvas 18″ x14″)

Each culture attempts to wrap a common truth in its own colours.

THESE ARE A FEW OF MY FAVOURITE THINGS
(Oil on canvas 12″ x18″)

After getting some of the deeper issues off my chest I thought I'd paint some of my favourite things. Coves on the Balearics, games of mental agility, games of chance, winning, and cherries and, of course, Cristina.

LEAVING THE CIRCUS
(Oil on canvas 12″ x16″)

I had a dream, many years ago, one of those dreams which you don't forget.

My dream was set at night. Attracted by manic laughter coming from outside, I went to an open window, where a clown suddenly appeared. The clown was chewing a match, which he spat through the window opening, hitting me in the chest. When I looked down there was a splatter of blood where the match had hit me.

My interpretation is that I am the clown who wishes to escape the circus, the rat race. The spat match and the blood – perhaps that is the acknowledgement of my being a part of that circus, of my complicity with the ringmaster. I believe that only the dreamer can interpret his or her dream. The information is so personal that it must be so. The psychologist Carl Jung saw that while we are in the relaxed state of sleep, just as in deep meditation, we glimpse our connection to the unity of the whole. Our dreams are that unity's communication with our physical being.

PHOEBE

I wasn't brought up with pets. Mother had a budgie called George, which was the same name as my father. I often wondered about that – why call a pet the same name as your partner?

When George, the budgie, passed away at the ripe old age of thirteen he was replaced by a budgie chick, a Christmas present from one of mother's friends. This new arrival didn't do anywhere near as well as his predecessor.

For some reason it dropped from its perch that very day during the Christmas edition *of Top of the Pops.* Perhaps it was Noddy Holder screaming It's Chrisssssstmas. - I don't know. But that was the end of pets – unless you count the goldfish we won at Grey's travelling fair, which visits nearby Blakeney every summer. Sadly the trauma of transportation in plastic bags dangling from bicycle handlebars was quite often too much for them, and on the rare occasions when they did survive the journey and manage to settle into their new environment, they would then proceed, at their leisure, to eat one another.

Either way, proper pets such as dogs and cats were always dismissed by George the father, a bricklayer and true local, as filthy creatures whose cost far outweighed any pleasures they could possibly bring.

Father's influence and the large black mongrel that made my paper round a nightmare had me leaning towards the

☼☺

anti-dog camp. That final push to dog hater came during the summer of my thirteenth year. Having just started secondary school, one of my new friends invited me to stay for the weekend. This was exciting stuff. Family holidays weren't something we did. I vaguely remember a week in Lowestoft and being lost on Cromer pier, but this was different. For the first time in my life I would be on my own.

Matthew, my friend, lived about 12 miles along the coast to the west in an old farmhouse at Holkham. They were quite a large family and subsequently, come bedtime, I found myself trying to get to sleep on the couch in their dining room. The imposing antique furniture and the areas of impenetrable darkness gave the room an eerie atmosphere that was not conducive to sweet dreams. More than that, it was the solid tick and chime on the hour and half hour of the ornate mantel clock that put even a short snooze out of the question.

At half past two I was tired, awake, fed up and in such a strange house – the stair well was papered with the pages from a wallpaper book – that out of desperation I decided to stop the clock's pendulum. I would then start it again before the rest of the house awoke. With this done I managed a few hours restless sleep and felt quite smug as I re-set the hands and started the clock later that morning. This was short-lived, as during cereal the clock struck three! In a move that might have been choreographed to perfection, the family in unison turned to look at the priceless heirloom, their faces caught between shock and concern. As the certain realisation hit them that I had a hand in the clock's confused state, they all turned to me. I opened my mouth but nothing came. Nauseous with embarrassment, I dropped my head and stared at my soggy cornflakes. There followed an awkward silence that lasted the rest of breakfast. I was glad to be out of that house into the morning sunshine. Matthew laughed as I told him what I'd done to the clock. We met other friends from school, we went to the beach, just hung out, lazing about in the dunes, but best of all, we were in the company of girls. It was great.

Since then I often wonder why such emotional highs have to be smashed against the rocks of reality so hard, and yes, I've done the "a problem is a gift for us to learn from" thing, but at the age of thirteen all I could see was disaster. The smell first brought it to my notice. I obviously hadn't paid enough attention to father' s warnings about the filth, as he called it, that dogs leave behind. If I had perhaps I wouldn't now have been looking at it smeared across the knee of my jeans.

The embarrassment of proclaiming the catastrophe was too great; I discreetly removed as much as possible from these, the only trousers I'd brought with me, by rubbing the offending knee in sand and on the grass but there was no disguising the smell.

First the clock and now this; I returned home to Wiveton that day.

Matthew was never invited to stay at our house. Not only did father not like pets, he didn't care too much for other people's children either.

Cristina, however was brought up with dogs and knew it was the irresponsible owners that were the problem. She had seen the up side of having these peculiar little friends. Her understanding nature is full of forgiveness. I once listened in disbelief as she recalled stepping bare-foot across her parents' stone kitchen floor. She described it as squishing like putty between her toes. Such powers of forgiveness.

Understanding that they give back far more than they demand, she waited patiently for me to work through my dog phobia while being the parent of two young children. She waited patiently as I became accustomed to our friends' dogs and her parents' dogs – Boston Terriers which have to be the ugliest of breeds. She waited until she knew I could take it before gently suggesting that, "Maybe we could consider getting a dog?" Worn away like a pebble in a stream, I told myself it would make Cristina happy but in truth I had come to like certain dogs, and was now quite excited about the prospect of owning one.

We decided we wanted a pedigree that looked like a loveable rogue, something with a long coat. Perhaps a Bearded Collie we thought, but couldn't find one for love or money. The Spinone, an Italian hound, looked good but, being a hound, its mouth was continuously running with drool, not a pretty sight. Hoping for inspiration we watched Crufts on television and spotted a Polish Lowland Sheepdog bouncing across the arena.

Similar to the Bearded Collie but with no tail the Lowland is quite a new breed to this country. Consequently its breeders are very protective. I would talk to them for an hour on the telephone until I had won their confidence, only to be told that they had no puppies to sell; they would, however, give me the name of someone who might have, and then the whole vetting process would begin again. We were passed around like this until we found a chap in Grimsby, who would have a litter ready in about three months. At last we were put on a list of possibly suitable owners.

We followed the bitch's progress, and eventually we got the summons to view the litter with the understanding that, if he thought we were suitable, we could return in six weeks and hand over a small fortune.

The Humber Bridge. What a wonderful piece of engineering. We had a picnic on the bank under its great towers and cables, and then proceeded to see the puppies that were just a few miles down the road.

At the gate of a row of semis just off a busy roundabout we were greeted by three Lowlands and their master, who didn't fit the enquiring telephone voice at all. Like the breed he had a caring laid-back attitude which made us immediately feel at home.

After some small talk and further subtle vetting, he almost casually told us we could pick one of the three remaining pups of the litter of five.

The mother proudly nursed the fat snuffley creatures that blindly rolled around searching for milk. Watching them I couldn't help think of the despair she would feel as she watched them leave one by one. As to which to choose, we had neither the knowledge nor experience to base our choice on anything other than sex, colour and marking. The children loved them. It was difficult not to, and the decision was unanimous. We would reserve the white and black bitch.

Driving home to *Broadview*, the car was buzzing and all the time I'm caught between 'Oh God; what have I done!' and contributing suggestions for names. Before we reached Wiveton we had narrowed the list down to Lileth or Phoebe, both characters from the Friday night American soaps. There were some reservations about standing in the garden calling, Lileth, so we decided it would be Phoebe who we would return to Grimsby for in six weeks' time.

All puppies are adorable and Phoebe was no exception. She was just what I imagined she would be, and more. Within six weeks she had ruined every carpet in the house. She had actually done us a favour because none of them were anything other than £1.99 per sq yd cords. They were already old, and I had come to hate the feel of the nylon on my bare feet. Beneath them lay clean 80-year-old floorboards. A bit draughty but beautiful when sanded and varnished.

Phoebe had her little piece of fenced garden, which prevented her exploring too far and getting lost, but as soon as she had been immunised we were ready to go out walking in the big wide world.

Being reasonably early risers means most places are deserted when we set out, and living on the North Norfolk coast, there isn't a shortage of walks through woods, fields, heaths, marshes and of course the beach. All have their particular beauty changing through the seasons. There's always a walk and it's always the right one.

When you're out early in the day your senses and feelings are at their most intense. Your mind is clear of the complications that pile up during the course of the day. Your body is rested. It's a great time as the old cliché says for "getting in touch with yourself".

Although all the countryside has its story to tell I am continually drawn to the beach at Cley. Standing on the top of the shingle bank the 360 degree view gives one the sense of being part of something very special.

Covered mostly in smooth pebbles of varying size, its form changes with the intensity of the sea's condition but on the whole it shelves steeply revealing a strip of hard sand, at low tide, which makes walking far easier than on the constantly shifting pebbles.

To the east lie Sheringham and Cromer, to the west is a narrow spur of land running parallel to the coast which has built up from deposits of sand moved from the east by the action of wind and the currents.

This spur of land is Blakeney Point and is only accessible along Cley beach, or by the boats from Blakeney and nearby Morston.

To the north is the North Sea, sometimes as flat and peaceful as a mirror, its surface only disturbed by the seals and diving birds, at other times a wild and churning threat to anyone who ventures near it.

To the south, about a mile across the salt marsh, are Cley, Wiveton and Blakeney. Running along the back of the beach is the outlet of the River Glaven. Its source is the fresh water springs that surface a few miles inland and flow out meeting the tidal salt-water at Cley, which then snakes its way through the marsh and out to the estuary and the sea.

Early mornings down at the beach are wonderful. There is no one for miles. Phoebe explores the marshes and I have time to explore my thoughts and feelings and to notice the natural world. There are always interesting things washed ashore. Sometimes after a storm large timbers from ships wrecked, who knows when and under what circumstance, arrive amongst every form of plastic wrapper you can imagine. Syringes, spent lighters and fish crates, you name it, it gets washed up.

Having been born and lived all my life on a coast prone to flooding, I was aware of the rhythm of the tides and their twelve-and-a-half hour interval, although I knew little more than that they were caused by the Moon's gravitational pull on the Earth this being at its greatest at the full and new Moon.

When the Moon is full it is obvious because it's up there in the night sky for all to see, but it was when it shows up as a crescent, referred to as the waxing Moon, that I first begin to notice the subtle ways in which the Moon influences me.

While walking on the beach with Phoebe, I noticed the waxing Moon could be seen quite clearly during the day. Nothing fantastic about that, I hear you say, but after spotting the Moon month after month at this part of its cycle, I began to notice an obvious coincidence. Whenever this waxing Moon was in the sky I always felt good. It's as simple as that. It always caught me in an upbeat mood, feeling that anything was possible. I'd be strolling along just feeling on top of the world – and there it was.

At the time I thought nothing of it, but then we take so many of the things that happen in the natural world for granted. For instance, which way does the world turn in relation to the sun in this our Northern Hemisphere?

I had put to the back of my mind the fact that we are spinning through space covering hundreds of miles an hour. It really is a smooth ride don't you think? The sun does appear to rise but we all know that in fact it is we that sweep past it without fail every day.

Eventually I stopped thinking of the association of the waxing Moon and my state of mind as a coincidence; it has become a fact of life for me that the two are in some way linked. Why shouldn't they be? After all, the word lunatic derives from just such a connection. And if the force of gravity can move great bodies of water, then I see no reason why it shouldn't have a more subtle effect on us humans.

Such wonders and my thoughts of the Moon went to another level when, much to Phoebe's excitement, we bought a boat.

Incidentally, the Earth turns anti-clockwise. As does everything in our solar system; or as my good friend and editor of this book, John Sykes, reasons, as the Earth was here before the clock, shouldn't it be that, clocks turn anti Earth-wise?

FLAMINGO

Sports Day was one of the dates on the school calendar that as a parent I had come to dread, Christmas pantomimes being another one. Cristina is certain Benylin secretly sponsors the panto on account of its being a breeding ground for flu just before the holidays.

Sports day isn't looked forward to by our daughter, Emily, either. Not being a natural athlete, she would take part but never enjoy it.

The last two races are always for the parents. It's pay back time. The child is relentlessly coerced by a bearded teacher with a bullhorn to drag their protesting parents on to the track. The previous year I was saved from this ritual humiliation by a faller at the back of the field in the ladies race. The resulting broken shoulder blade put an end to that year's proceedings, but twelve months on I found myself standing by the same track chatting to some friends about the small boat which they keep at Cley, in the process trying desperately to avoid eye contact with the headmaster or Emily.

Cristina and I had often talked of getting a boat so we were genuinely interested, and Ray always seemed to know of a boat that was 'just what you re looking for'.

Today was no exception. As we talked he described *Flamingo,* a 14 foot glass fibre boat on a swinging mooring. This meant you had to tie up wherever you could, at

♀☺

Cley Mill. At £125, complete with outboard and trailer, it was in our price bracket, so we decided to take a look at it after school, which was in fact "now". Caught up in the excitement of buying into the boating fraternity we had missed the last race.

We went directly to Cley to look *Flamingo* over. At low tide this salt-water side of the River Glaven is nothing more than a muddy creek, but your attention is usually distracted by the imposing Mill that looks out over the Quay. This same Mill also adorns just about every tourist souvenir sold in the area.

Today our attention was focused on the mud splattered *Flamingo*. She was basic and pink. I can only presume the name came from the colour, and the colour came from the leftovers of a decorated bedroom. Next we went to the owner's house. He was in the process of selling up. We knew each other vaguely and managed to piece together events and people from the past before working our way around to the outboard. He didn't disguise the fact that it wasn't much good and that he was giving it to us. That understood, we shifted our attention to a rusty old road trailer, a couple of pairs of oars and various bits and bobs that were all part of the deal. The only thing left to consider was whether we wanted it.

Embarking into any new field you're bound to make a few mistakes. It's a bit like buying your first car. You can't help but get caught up in the excitement, and for that reason you don't see the wreck and hours of work that are actually sitting there.

I'm not suggesting the owner was trying to sell us some-thing other than what it was, but that perhaps we percei-ved it as more.

Anyway, hands were shaken, and within two hours of being virtually oblivious of our desire to be part of the boating set, we were in.

We cleaned *Flamingo* up and decided to leave her in the water for the rest of the season. This was around the middle of June, so we hoped there would be plenty of fine weather in which we could pursue our new leisure activity.

The engine was on its last legs. We didn't realise how much on its last legs until we fitted it to the boat. Another little curiosity about it was that the propeller was the wrong thread. This meant that the first time we started it – we went backwards!

Ray lent us a propeller that would send us in the desired direction. We mixed our oil and petrol. All we needed was a fine day and reasonable tide.

I had grown up in the marshes around the mill. It had been our playground for many a summer until other attractions enticed us away. Friends from those early days had boats, so I was used to falling in and getting muddy. All the same we were very grateful to Ray, who kindly chaperoned us on our first few outings.

Although we must have looked very clumsy and uncoor-dinated, the feel of the boat, the smells and sounds all brought wonderful memories flooding back to me.

Lulled into a false sense of security I decided it was time – we were ready to go out on our own, which of course was what the engine had been waiting for. It always did smoke a bit and it was noisy, but it was old, so you could forgive it that. We followed the course of the river winding through the marshes down to the beach, where we had a walk and a cup of tea from our flask. Everything was peachy. We returned to *Flamingo,* started the engine and headed home against the tide. We didn't get a hundred yards before it cut out. There then followed half an hour of adjusting the engine, trying to coax it into life, and getting hotter, greasier and more stressed with each fruitless pull of the cord.

We were on the point of giving in and walking home, when Ray appeared around the bend in the river, beaming from ear to ear as usual. "I thought that engine might play up", he remarked. I was just glad to see him and, while thankful for the rescue, there are few things as demoralising as being towed by another boat. Unfortunately, it was a feeling we would be well accustomed to by the end of September.

I tried every combination of carburettor setting, mixtures, sparkplugs, incantations, swearing and cursing, yet it still dumped us halfway, leaving us to make our own hot and disillusioned way home.

When a couple of months of breakdowns began to dull our initial enthusiasm, we decided that a must for boating has to be a reliable engine. This necessity was confirmed a few days later in a dramatic cloud of smoke, in which alas the Johnson four was no more.

Ray happened to have a Mariner four which he suggested was probably just what we were looking for, and it was. We could just get in the boat, go out, and come back.

Something all the other boat owners had done all season. You didn't have to break down, and from that point boating became pure relaxation, maybe there was something we had to learn. Having an engine that works seems fairly obvious now, but perhaps there was a test of endurance in there somewhere.

At the beginning of next year's season, around March time, I helped Ray build an extension on his bungalow, and one day, out of the blue, he gave us a fine jetty as a thank you present. He's like that.

With Ray's help we brought *Flamingo* back to *Broadview* for a re-fit. Cristina chose yellow and white for the outside and blue and white for the inside. How that was going to fit with the boat being named after a large pink bird, I wasn't sure, but we let it go, as apparently it's bad luck to re-name a vessel.

We put a new seat in and had her back in the water within a week. We were established. We had a good jetty, a reasonable boat and a reliable engine.

Our lives began to revolve around a little book called a tide timetable. Set out like a calendar, it shows the heights and times of the tides for each day of the year.

Tides are governed by the gravitational pull of the Moon and to a lesser extent that of the Sun. The Earth's water bulges at the point closest to the Moon, while on the opposite side of the planet a similar size bulge appears due to the unequal tension on the planet's water surface created by the centrifugal force exerted by the spinning Earth. A bit of a mouthful but as you may have guessed, I had become interested in the forces at work here.

The highest tides occur at the New Moon and the Full Moon; these are called spring tides. New Moons occur when the Sun and Moon are almost in line so their combined gravitational pull heaps up a lot of water, they work in conjunction. At the Full Moon, the Moon and Sun are at opposite sides of the planet, exerting the same force but working in opposition.

The lowest tides of the Moon's cycle occur when the Moon and Sun have the least gravitational pull on the Earth, which is when the Moon and Sun are at a 90-degree angle to the Earth. These are called neap tides.

Full Moons are fascinating and mysterious, the silver light replacing fears of darkness with serenity and balance. The dogs howl, lunatics loon and we go boating.

The spring tides at the New and Full Moon allow you. more time out. You're also up much higher at marsh level as the river is full to overflowing. Now able to take in the scenery, it's easy to drift back in time, as a great deal of history has made the same journey.

Once a busy port navigable up to Wiveton, the Glaven has seen many large ships at her quays. In 1612 the warehouses and much of the village of Cley were a mile further inland near the Church at Newgate, but after a great fire were relocated closer to the mill. The river's demise came in 1637, when landowners tried to reclaim parts of the marsh by building a bank across the main channel. After two years of protests in the high courts by the people and businesses whose livelihoods had been lost the government ordered that the bank should be removed. The channel relied on the spring tides to flush the silt out and after being denied this for two years the damage was done. The port never recovered, and neither did the river trade and prosperity.

There must be a number of old ships that once visited Cley and Wiveton wrecked and lying on the bottom. On occasions after storms large timbers are dislodged and thrown up on the beach.

One bleak morning I happened upon just such a piece. The problem was how to get it home. With the help of my father I rolled it a bit at a time over the beach and into the river. From there we towed it behind *Flamingo* to the quay at Cley where we hauled it out with a J.C.B. and put it on the back of my pick-up.

It sounds easy, but on the day both time and tide were against us in that we were running out of both daylight and water. The weight of the timber had it floating below the surface where it continually dug into the bottom, almost pulling the stern out of *Flamingo*. The luck we'd had so far was pushed to the extreme when the digger, now working using its spotlight, had just lifted the huge timber clear of the water. The rope holding it broke. The timber slid back down the bank, but stopped half in half out of the water where we could just get to it with a chain. We were meant to have it, and in the end we did.

It's a marvellous piece of timber, some 14 feet long and 14 inches square and has pride of place over the inglenook at *Broadview*. I often picture it coming up the channel in Wiveton's glory days, perhaps the main timber in some fine sailing ship.

Flamingo settled into a routine of outings that might sound unexciting. We go out and come back down the same stretch of river, but it's enough for us, it's relaxing, good for the soul. Every once in a while we'll embark on an adventure to Morston or Blakeney Point. We chase kingfishers down the creek and drift into sunsets so still you can't tell where the sky ends and the water begins.

Over the years we progressed up the boating ladder to *Eos* (Goddess of morning), a bigger and faster boat, although we still have *Flamingo* – and always will.

READING THE CARDS

Pete and Liz Sanderson live in Northumberland. They've been coming to stay with us since we first opened. Pete is a keen birdwatcher, so keen that he has a pager which tells him what rarities have been sighted and where. Not keen as in "twitcher". These are birders who seem to be interested in bird spotting almost as a competition.

Before coming to us they had rented another holiday cottage in Wiveton situated very close to the river Glaven. So close in fact that on their two previous stays the drains had backed up with flooding from the river and they had to use the ablutions in the owner's house. Not ideal, so it was our good fortune that they came to us.

Unfortunately for Pete and Liz, their first visit was the week of the petrol strike, and so, to be certain they had enough fuel to get back to Northumberland they left their car in the yard all week. As we got to know them it became apparent that they were no strangers to holidays disturbed by events beyond their control. A couple of months earlier they had been on the Isle of Harris when the ferries went on strike so they had had to cut short their holiday to avoid being stranded.

The next time they came to stay with us, having booked months in advance, was at the outbreak of the foot and mouth crisis, which shut all the bird reserves. Although the weather was atrocious with high winds and sleet, Pete

♂♀

would go down to the Cley reserve and look into it from the shingle bank along its northern boundary, or from the mud bank to the east. On one particular day few were brave enough to face the conditions. After an hour or so the biting northerly had chilled Pete to the bone and so he returned to his car. In a steamed up Land Cruiser, waiting for the weather to break, several birders were sitting, one of whom rolled down his window to see what was about. "You're keen", they taunted, as they sipped steaming beverage from their thermos cups. Pete laughed. "I've got to make the most of things, wherever I go catastrophe seems to strike". With that the chap in the car recoiled away from Pete, and turned to his passenger to exclaim, "Oh God, it's that bloke from Northumberland!" and without another word, wound up his window. Clearly Pete's notoriety had spread throughout the birding community. The funny thing is that Pete's tales of woe are always told with a positive spirit, where every cloud has a silver lining. He approaches every situation with a smile on his face, embracing whatever life throws at him.

On one occasion a bee-eater, a small colourful bird which apparently is a rarity in this country, appeared on the shoreline of Northumberland. Pete was paged and made his way to where the exhausted bird had last been sighted. The end of the beach road was clogged by a mass of deserted vehicles, the owners of which were moving in a straggled out band along the shore. There followed a two-mile walk before Pete caught up with the crowd of 60 or more birders. They had spotted the bee-eater in a patch of dense low bushes, where it had disappeared from view. It seemed that it hadn't occurred to the gathered enthusiasts that the terrified creature was hiding from them, if it had, then perhaps they wouldn't have begun the systematic beating of the bushes in order to locate it, on the other hand, perhaps it had, and they just didn't care. Either way Pete wanted no part of it. He turned round and walked back to his car and went home disgusted at what he'd seen.

Pete is a retired policeman who now works for a charity that looks after children who've had a bad time, I'm sure you know what I mean. Pete organises holidays for them at outward-bound centres, which the charity owns. One of these centres is a working farm that incorporates a disused quarry. Over the years the staff there have turned this quarry into a small nature reserve where, the day after his experience with the over enthusiastic birders, not one but two bee-eaters arrived. They spent the next few months nesting in the quarry, where they successfully raised a brood. Pete spent a couple of months camped out there to make certain the birds weren't disturbed, it was one of the best kept RSPB secrets of 2002.

But this story isn't about Pete; it's about his wife Liz.

Liz and Pete had been round for a cup of tea and, as they left, Liz was drawn to one of my paintings hanging in the hall. It's a view from an upstairs apartment looking out across a street towards a diner. The waitress of the diner is standing outside contemplating life beyond her dreary world, but that's all beside the point, the thing is that Liz spotted the ladybird. I had painted it on the windowsill, to fill a glaringly empty space in the foreground of the picture.

She wondered if I used the insect as a trademark, which I don't but, as I said, that's all irrelevant. The relevance of the ladybird didn't become apparent until the end of the year.

We like to decorate the house at Christmas time, not lines and lines of flashing lights and plastic Santas, it's "all done in the best possible taste", and the last things to go up are the cards. This is ritually done on Christmas Eve. The operation involves lengths of string pinned to the beams. The strings reach almost to the floor, weighted down by stones with holes in them. The cards are then paper-clipped to these strings. To add an element of depth, the strings are hung away from the walls. Cristina thinks I'm going too far with it but – it's Christmas. Anyway, as I clip each card on, I read who it's from. Pete and Liz's card had a picture of birds sitting on a snow covered washing line. These birds diminish in size from a starling down to a wren, and inside Liz had written "I hope you like the card". I thought it obviously a reference to Pete's love of birding, so, yes, I liked the card.

As I began clipping it to the string, I looked beyond the job in hand to where a ladybird was walking across the wall. Still holding Liz's card, I instantly recalled her noticing the ladybird on the picture in our hall.

Now would be a good time to point out that my eyesight is not so good for close up work, I really should wear spectacles. I tingled as I squinted my eyes to look really closely at the card and there, next to the wren on the snow covered line, was a ladybird.

This is the day before Christmas and there is a ladybird walking across the wall of our lounge! What are the chances of these events coinciding? Millions to one! Coincidence? I don't think so.

At the beginning of February Pete phoned to book a week in March. I was stunned to hear, upon asking if they'd had a good Christmas, that sadly Liz's mother had died on Christmas Eve, and what made matters worse, Christmas Eve was Liz's birthday.

Such intensely personal experiences and the quality of the emotions they evoke demonstrate that a connection between all things must exist. The odds of such happenings being coincidental are incalculable. What's more, once this flow of synchronicity is accepted and we learn to cooperate with it, to "go with the flow", then life becomes a lot less stressful. Of course, that's speaking from experience and, being creatures blessed with the gift of free will, we require proof. That's why I set out to find a scientific, material explanation for such happenings.

Spirits In The Material World

While immersed in the natural world, out walking with Phoebe or boating, that's when I most sense a harmony between all things. On such occasions the stress and concerns of the everyday world are virtually non-existent. Many people choose to opt out of the rat race in favour of embracing this connection, but few to such an extent as one Susan Dean. Susan lives unplugged, as she calls it, in a log cabin, which she and her husband built amongst 63 acres of woodlands in the Adirondak Mountains, New York State. With no telephone or electrical appliances Susan really does feel the pulse of the planet. We can't all go and live up a mountain in such harmony, but we all find escapes, even in our hectic 21st century lives. We lose ourselves in our hobbies and pastimes, which allow us to forget the stresses that are heaped upon us. We dream. At other times flashes of synchronicity provide answers to our questions. The questions are quite often never spoken, they are just a puzzle which we are trying to solve in our heads and then, when we least expect it, "bang" the answer is right before us, in what some people might call a flash of coincidence. The connection is made and the puzzle answered. This unity of all things and its implication has always been a puzzle to me, so much so that a few years ago I decided to look into how this connection was possible.

♂Ψ

There are libraries full of books offering guidance in this matter. The formula is generally the same and seems, quite simply, to advise that you put aside the material and self-centred cravings which cause the stresses that dull the senses. This act of contrition and the focus of meditation free your physical being and allow it to sense the connection. These books tell us how to find "the way", but they don't give us a scientific explanation and this was what I was looking for.

There is a problem that confronts anyone trying to broach subjects of such a sensitive nature. You've only got to mention particular watch words concerning an omnipotent force, and people tend to close up. This is understandable, but makes it difficult to open a debate on the subject, which is sad, as the fragility of our brief mortality is constantly used as an emotional lever in this material world, and therefore is a matter which is quite often on our minds.

So, to the search for a scientific explanation. I found a book on the subject by an American scientist, Valerie Hunt, who had explored the aura of energy emitted by the human body. For us to exist beyond our physical being, I supposed that it would have to be as a frequency, a vibration, and so this line of investigation seemed as good a place as any to start. By breaking the frequencies into different levels and cross-referencing these through statistical analyses, Dr Hunt could interpret the readings to the mental, physical and spiritual characteristics of the subject.

I decided to try and copy this experiment but to do this I would need a helper, for when all is said and done, I can wire a plug and put up the Christmas tree lights, but my track record beyond that is shocking, literally!

I enlisted the help of an American named Stephen Coop. I found Coop, as he liked to be called, through the good old free ads newspaper, in which I asked if there was anybody out there who could help me make an old-fashion crystal set radio. Why so? Well, these old radios picked up frequencies, radio waves, out of the air using a long piece of copper wire as an aerial. This aerial was attached to a crystal (a piece of galena) which then reso-nated to that frequency. When stroked with a thin piece of wire (a cat's whisker) these frequencies or vibrations were fed to headphones where they became the audible sound which had originally been broadcast. Coop sat on the edge of his seat as he enthused about how, 50 years ago, he had made simple galena crystal sets. He was one of three people to reply to my ad, and living less than a mile from *Broadview* made him the obvious first choice. Jovial and intense, curious and interesting, this mild-mannered man was in his mid sixties, short and carrying a few pounds but nothing disastrous. His round specta-cled face smiled a lot, the wrinkled jowls pulling large lips into a giant grin.

Having established that Coop was capable of helping me, the next step was to put to him the reason why I wanted to make a crystal set. I realised that my talking about trying to find a link between man giving out an aura, and how that aura connected with everything else in the universe, might have some folk running for the door but Coop liste-ned quietly, dismissing nothing as impossible.

After an hour the talk of the crystal set was long forgotten. The idea of making such a machine had captured Coop's imagination, and he was certainly open-minded enough to believe that such forces exist.

The eldest brother of a large Boston family, Coop was unfortunate enough to have to shoulder the responsibility of becoming the head of the family at an early age. Working as a provider rather than attending college made Coop's dreams of employment in the electronics industry difficult, until his time in the army allowed him to become a radar operator and technician. During the Second World War this work brought him to England, where he met and married his wife. On their return to the States Coop found employment with the Massachusetts Institute of Technology, where his work was mainly subcontracted to the government's space programme.

As I listened, the table had been turned. I'd been afraid that Coop would dismiss my interest as an impossible dream of romantic nonsense, but as he told me of his work for N.A.S.A. an edge of scepticism crept into my thoughts. Coop told me he had been one of the technicians who had been responsible for building the gyroscopic guidance system that put man on the moon back in 1969.

I had hoped to meet someone who could build a crystal set radio. The man sitting before me asked me to believe he was a rocket scientist.

Coop talked at length about the astronauts he'd met, the rockets he'd worked on, landing vehicles, space technology, it all fascinated me, then overwhelmed me until I found myself questioning his authenticity. The fact was, I had only met him an hour or so ago. I'd asked him if he'd like to help me make a machine which would show how we continue beyond and after our physical form, and he'd answered: "Sure. After all, my previous employer asked me to put a man on the moon"!

The meeting was surreal, and as I waved goodbye and watched him amble off down the track that leads from *Broadview* I had to remind myself, anything is possible, keep an open mind.

Over the next 18 months Coop and I would meet once or twice a week in the office at his house, where he would work long into the night, choosing to sleep during the day. Coop's work was on occasions interrupted by migraine headaches, which he had been prone to all his life. At the outbreak of one of these attacks Coop would retreat into a darkened room for a week or so until he had recovered.

Any doubts as to his authenticity or capability were dispelled by space agency reports from the sixties, which praised his work, and by his prized photographs, which showed him as an obvious friend and colleague of several famous American astronauts.

Coop had read through the book written by Dr Hunt and had dismissed it as being of no scientific value. The technical information and procedures she had used were vague at best, her data and graphs incomplete.

We supposed that these omissions were intentional, in order to safeguard years of costly research, but it meant that we would have to start from scratch following the outline of her procedure.

Using an oscilloscope we monitored the body's energy at skin level using sensors like the ones used in hospitals. Then by amplifying the frequencies and filtering them into bands, we hoped to compile our own database from which we could indicate trends enabling us to interpret our readings.

The progress was painfully slow. Coop's adherence to the scientists' creed that findings are worthless unless backed by solid, tried and tested procedure and technical data, meant that nothing was taken for granted or left to chance. Just when I thought we'd made progress, Coop would find another quite valid reason to apply another test. It began to dawn on me that to attempt what I had in mind was like a mouse having a go at building a grandfather clock. A more disturbing side of the project was that Coop's headaches were becoming more frequent and intense. At the end of the winter of 1998 I received the phone call from him saying that due to ill health he would have to stop work on the project. Frustrated by our lack of progress, I conceded defeat and began to consider what I had learned from this particular outing.

On the technical side of things, what struck me the most was the extent to which our bodies pick up extraneous electromagnetic frequencies. When monitoring body energy, the oscilloscope readings were affected by any electrical apparatus, even the house lighting circuit. To prevent these frequencies distorting our readings, the person being monitored had to be shielded by being enclosed in an insulated box. As to whether the energy we picked up related to any physical, mental or spiritual condition, I couldn't say for certain. I would like to think they did, but Coop could always find a reason why they might not, which would have to be checked. This took us deeper and deeper into the pure electronic systems of amplifiers and filters that he created.

Coop's art is science, where there is never an answer, only the next question. Any theory is just that – a theory and it waits to be superseded.

Using his most powerful telescopes man looks way out to the edge of our known universe, and with his electron microscopes he looks deep within every cell of our being. However there is a limit to where man can go. That limit is himself. In the years to come I realised that the energy which connects all things is so subtle that the act of looking for it always contaminates the search. If you think about it logically, a description of anything requires, by implication, that the person who is "describing" be separate from the subject matter. The true experience of anything can only be known while we experience "being it", while we are "one with it".

If you look too closely at a newspaper picture, all you will see is lots of little dots. Looking at one of those dots was what I was doing with Coop, and during that time I never felt further away from being part of the "big picture." I would enthuse to my friend Ray how wonderful our machine would be, and how we would prove our existence beyond our physical being. In truth it was nothing more than a dreamer's theory. It never had that "wow!" feeling that accompanies an undeniable truth as it becomes clear throughout our entire being. That split second, which is forever, in which the path to our realisation unifies in the pure place within us all, where there is no need for further questions and answers.

I had failed to find a scientific explanation, but all around me in a society so discontent with itself was made manifest a multitude of reasons why I should keep looking. What's more, everything pointed to the fact that the explanation I sought would come from observations of the "bigger picture", so I decided that that's where I would look next.

Inevitably with failure there comes disappointment and frustration, which is expressed in the following picture:

THE WATCH-HOUSE
(Oil on canvas 24″ x36″)

The watch-house is a building halfway between Cley Beach and Blakeney Point.

Its remote position makes it ideal for contemplation.

Why we are here, where we are from, and where do we go from here, etc, etc. We look for answers, which are under our very noses, should we but care to see them. Instead we choose to look away. Yet we find ourselves at the same place over and over again, asking the same questions, when the answers are simply the truths which we don't want, or at least, truths which we are yet unable to accept. Clues to our conundrum appear as riddles in the least expected places, pointing us to answers that we must find for ourselves. Until we recognise these messengers, they appear as surreal as the Cheshire Cat in Alice in Wonderland.

THE HALL OF LIFE
(The case for keeping your mouth shut)

Truth is like a crystal chandelier that hangs in the hall of life. We all see it, but because all paths through life are different, we all see it from a different point of view. We each deal as best we can with the truth of conscience which wells up inside us. Some die upholding it, others are not so strong.

One person stands to the far left as he passes through the hall. This person uses analytical logic to avoid facing his truth. He loses himself in the routine and the public relation pump which spews from every surface open to manipulation. He occupies himself so he doesn't have to look within. He becomes robotic.

The person to the far right uses one of the many addictions available to anaesthetise himself against this breakdown of the 21st Century, in the hope that the synthetic hit will allow one brief moment of being at one with his truth.
He becomes as weightless and drifting as a balloon.
They both see the light.
The person standing in the middle of the room is in awe of the light that streams down from the chandelier, but of it he cannot tell. It is his truth, and everyone's truth is different. Each according to their point of view.

SELF PORTRAIT
(The case for opening it.)

From Blakeney Point looking back across the estuary towards Blakeney. A beautiful day spent out boating. Sitting on the shoreline with Cristina, I became aware that around us, in their boats, were a completely random, unconnected selection of truly local people who fascinate me. A major landowner, an artist and a solicitor. These people occupy the picture that is being played out before me; but Cristina and I are there, on this beautiful day, and we are just as much a part of their picture as they are of ours.

It is our choice what part we play in the picture. We play the cards we are given as best we can, but should never underestimate the picture we create.

NICK AND MARTHA

All of our guests are interesting but just before Christmas
2003 a very interesting, as in out of the ordinary, couple
came to stay. They flew in from the other side of the
world, Toronto, arriving at Heathrow late in the evening.
It was 1.30 in the morning before they got to *Broadview*.
We decided that as they were making such an enormous
journey, we would stay up to see them in. Their hire car, a
Ford Ka, pulled tentatively into the drive and I went out to
meet them. As I approached it was immediately obvious
that the car was filled with people, actually two people.
The window wound down and an enormous head crowned
by a mass of long grey curly hair poked out, and as they
introduced themselves, I couldn't help but stare at the
long, thick beard which now dangled down the outside of
the door blowing in the wind.
They parked up and then unfolded themselves from the
groaning vehicle. Even with the seats back as far as they
would go it had obviously been a cramped journey.
Silhouetted by the outside light and with the wind billo-
wing their long green coats around them, Martha and Nick
made an impressive sight. They were huge, not fat but tall
and big, as opposed to being long and lanky, if you know
what I mean.
We showed them into *Hatter* and left them to settle in.
Over the next few days they came over for cups of tea and

♥☺

told us all about their adventures. The warmth and open-hearted way in which they embraced life made it really hard to guess their age. Their faces glowed in the firelight as they told their tales, taking you into the story with them. At such times you would have said, maybe, early fifties but when they talked of other matters their wisdom was timeless.

Nick had travelled the world working in all sorts of jobs; he'd even been stranded at Helsinki airport for a couple of hours with Michael Caine. Each country had its story but the one that sticks in my mind most clearly is the one about the time when he worked as a ranch hand in Tennessee.

When he had been a young man it was possible to travel from ranch to ranch earning your keep looking after the cattle, rounding them up, branding them and moving them from one grazing area to another. One hot summer he had arrived in a dusty one horse town, where the only shop open was the drug store. In order to find out who was hiring, and to rest and quench his thirst, Nick went in and bought a Coke. After getting the names of a couple of ranches from the bartender, and being the only person seated at the counter, he swivelled around so as to take in the view through the large window. After five minutes spent idly considering the beauty of the paint peeling architecture he realised that the pavements and the street outside were strangely empty. Turning back to the bartender, who was down the other end of the empty counter dusting glasses, Nick asked if it was always this quiet. The barman defended his store with vigour, saying it was a very well attended establishment – except, that is – when they're playing "the game." He was told that during the summer everyone attended the game on Sunday afternoons. It being Sunday afternoon, Nick thought little more of it until the following Saturday.

He had taken a job on the *Lone Star* ranch. It was a nice enough place, although the evenings had been a little lonely, as he was the only person staying in the large bunkhouse. The other cowhands lived in town or on the outskirts, so when the boss invited Nick over to eat at the main house that evening, he jumped at the chance of some company.

Over the course of dinner the boss raised a matter which, by the seriousness of his tone, was obviously of great importance to him.

One of the other hands, Jed, had fallen from his horse that morning and hurt his leg, and wouldn't be able to take part in the game the following day. As it was a needle match against their main contender in the league, it was important that they "rigged the ring with a full grid." Nick opened his mouth to explain that he had never heard of the game where he came from, and that he hadn't the faintest idea of how to rig any sort of ring. Before he could utter a syllable the boss continued "So, Nick, how'd you like to be Barn Jack tomorrow in Jed's place?" Nick hesitated for a moment as he considered his options. Firstly he didn't want to disappoint his host, secondly he didn't wish to appear stupid in front of the boss, thirdly it would be a golden opportunity to bond with the locals and fourthly ... it was too late. Nick had hesitated too long, which he realised as he heard the boss's voice interrupting his thoughts. "That's settled then. The playing ground's out beyond the silo, we kick off at 3 o'-clock." He then proceeded to explain the weaknesses and strengths of the two opposing sides. Strangely named players such as Corral Block, Can Man, Turkey Pen and Slow Dip took positions in a game which Nick tried to imagine in his head but eventually decided to wash away with another beer and try to find out the rules the following afternoon.

The next day was another scorcher just like they had been all month. With beads of sweat gathering on his brow, Nick approached the other players standing in the shadow of the silo. He told himself with all the confidence he could muster, that he would be able to wing it, but in truth the beads of sweat weren't entirely down to the heat.

Spectators' cars were forming a massive circle, which Nick supposed was the ring, the sunlight glinting off their windscreens and polished chrome.

Meanwhile the two camps of players were separated by an ever-decreasing space as they all attempted to remain within the shadow of the large galvanised silo, which looked out over the dust bowl where the game would be played.

The silence that prevailed suggested the gravity of the contest.

A coin was tossed. The winner, no less than the boss himself, turned and smiled at his grid (team), who answered it with a cheer as the opposing grid reluctantly stepped out of the cool shade into the blistering heat and headed out into the shimmering haze. The last two to leave the sanctuary of the shadow had been leaning back against the silo wall sitting on two 5-gallon oil drums, which they carried with them into the centre of the sun drenched arena, spacing them about the length of a cricket pitch apart.

Nick's nervous apprehension dissolved into a grin which grew and grew as before him in the Tennessee sunshine men dressed in denim dungarees and Stetson hats took up positions mirrored by men in crisp white linen shirts and trousers on village greens all over England.

Nick explained that between 1890 and 1900 an English teacher had worked in the local school. Being passionate about "the game" he had taught the pupils how to play. The pupils had grown up and moved out into the surrounding countryside where they in turn taught the game. These fledgling teachers used landmarks in their surroundings to give positions, "over there, by the barn, Jack" or "behind the can, man", and so the game evolved.

This was just one of Nick's stories, but after he left I started to think about it.

I had a funny feeling about this chap from the start.

He was big and jolly and exuded happiness and peace. He wore a long coat and had travelled halfway round the world from a country where reindeers live, he is called Nicholas, as in St Nicholas, as in Father Christmas, and to top it all, his wife is Martha an obvious reference to Mother Christmas.

Just as we are used to seeing cricketers dressed in whites and playing at slip, gully and silly-mid off we are also used to seeing Father Christmas dressed in a red coat trimmed with bands of white. Bear in mind the fact that the Coca-Cola Company introduced the red coat in the 30s, when they used Santa to promote their product. Previously to that Father Christmas was always depicted as wearing a long green coat. So it is that I seriously believe Father Christmas and Martha (Mother) Christmas came to stay with us that December.

The gift they shared with us was their positive spirit of love for all life and an exquisite box of chocolates, fair trade of course, which they left in *Hatter's* fridge.

We become so accustomed to the prescribed boundaries that our culture dictates, that sometimes it's hard to look outside the box, but that's all you have to do. Just a glimpse beyond – an altered perspective, and the walls just disappear.

THE THEORY

Why is it that we have to complicate everything? We take the simple and make a mystery of it. Before man came rushing out of the glory of his evolution with his liberating leap of consciousness everything was very simple, so simple he didn't even have to think about it. Pure energy connected everything and could be seen and felt as it flowed through all life in a harmonious dance so finely choreographed that all things worked in perfect sympathy. He simply knew he was a part of it.

Over thousands of years the inevitable evolution of man's brain forced him to break his link with that natural order. He began to think for himself, and in doing so took the pure and simple and turned it into a mystery that would occupy him for millennia to come.

Man's attempt to subjugate the natural order didn't happen over night, it took thousands of years. Changes over such lengths of time are usually imperceptible but so strong was man's connection and so dread was his loss that he kept his path to it open in his arts and in the building of massive monuments of stone. For the sake of the generations to come he knew that at all cost the link had to be maintained, for once it was gone there would be no way back.

The efforts to preserve the knowledge of that order are most dramatically seen in mega structures such as the

♥♠

stone circles. These certainly did their job, as today they act as a focus for the multitudes of people who once again are realising the perfect balance of that natural order, and are seeking to re-establish their connection to it.

There are libraries of books that attempt to help us find our way to that connection. These books come under various headings: mind, body and spirit, or religion, are obvious places to start, but as I said earlier, none of them are going to provide you with a simple, understandable answer. They offer deep and meaningful insights and plenty of snippets of wisdom, which are all very well in themselves, but go no way to explaining the whole thing, which seems rather strange, when only an explanation of the whole serves to answer all the questions.

Out of desperation you could go to the science shelves, where under astronomy you might pick up *'The Universe in a Nutshell'* by Professor Hawking. I imagined that "In a nutshell" implied something simplified but have you tried to make sense of that book?

Most folk who attempt an explanation of the mysteries of the universe pick a particular aspect, a category of mystery, to focus on, and that's where my theory is different; you see, this theory covers everything. Allow me to show you what I mean. Take, for instance, time travel; that's a topic we've become accustomed to by the likes of *Dr Who, Star Wars,* and *'The Time Machine'* by H.G. Wells; Here then, is "The theory Concerning the Existence of Time Travel." But it's also the theory that proves the existence of fairies and angels. It explains where we go to after death and where we came from before birth – everything, even the big one concerning His/Her Great Omnipotence!

Before we start there are some ground rules which must be observed. The first and foremost being one of the greatest paradoxes of them all.

Although we are dealing with a system that has the unity of all things as its core, we have to make our observations entirely from within ourselves. What I mean by this is that we can only make sense of the universe from our point of view. It's so easy to get side-tracked into imagining why other people are as they are, but that is no good, not in this book, so this is the first ground rule: the reasons behind what other people do, say or think are not our concern. Outside this book every aspect of life around us should indeed be our concern, but here the rules are different. Why monsters roam the planet preying on whom they will or why the sick and handicapped carry their heavy burden is not our concern. Our sole concern when we attempt to understand the unity can only be, strange as it might seem, ourselves. We can succeed in no other way. Why so? Because, as it is, we struggle with being honest with ourselves, we make all sorts of excuses for our weaknesses rather than admitting to them. So, as we find it so hard to be honest with ourselves and to understand ourselves, how can we hope to understand the complicated web of life experience which made others as they are? So Rule Number 1 is that we only think for ourselves, and that's enough of rules for the time being.

Now this idea didn't just come out of the blue with a "Bing". No, this was one of those ideas that needed a fair amount of contemplation. Also, I've found with ideas like this, that they never end up where you think they will, but take on a life of their own, dragging you along as an observer.

The concept can be simply presented using a glass ball about the size of an apple with a spiral expanding from its centre.

Wanting to check out my idea, I took it to a friend with a BSc. degree, with honours, in physics. To my joy he enthused about the theory and explained that it managed to clarify and encapsulate the workings of quantum physics in a way he had never before seen. This was a revelation to me and far more than I had hoped for. Up until that moment, I had considered knowledge of such things as quantum physics to be the domain of the selected few, who talked and expressed themselves in a foreign language which I don't understand!

The working of the theory shows that it is indeed possible that we exist in other dimensions, most importantly, even after what we perceive as the end of our physical life.

Now, as I have said before, I was getting into an area that most people are a little sensitive about. I've noticed that the vast majority of folk have a deep curiosity about the after-life, but ask for an opinion and the subject is taboo, they become defensive and back away quicker than if you'd asked to borrow a tenner. Bearing in mind the smallness of our community, and not wishing to have myself marked down as another poor soul who had obviously got himself "lost on the marshes", I decided I needed the support of a person of authority and who better than the Canon of our parish, the Reverend Philip Norwood?

Many generations of the Balding family have been baptised in the font at St Nicholas's Church, Blakeney. We all attended the C. of E. school that stands in its shadow, but that said, I am far from being a regular member of the congregation. I like to visit the church on occasion to marvel at the wonderful architecture. At these times I am always touched by the building's profound energy of peace and calm, but beyond that – no.

My last visit to the rectory had been several years earlier and had ended in disaster. The parson's wife, at the time, was a leader of the local sea scouts. She had the idea of using what she called the "snob value" of the rectory to get people to attend a tabletop sale to raise funds. What she meant was that people who wouldn't normally go to such a function would attend just to see the inside of the rectory.

Our son, Seth, was serving on one of the tables of bric-a-brac, so Cristina and I took Emily along. Just as had been expected, it was well attended, and the viewers' main interest wasn't the odds and ends laid out on the tables.

Upon arrival we were each given a steaming hot cup of coffee. I drink mine black. We then had carefully to negotiate our way through the throng whilst Emily, who was of an age when it is impossible to remain still for a second, danced along between us.

Our route was closed down by elderly shuffling tweed until the inevitable happened. Emily, while practising hopping from one leg to another, knocked my arm, spilling the boiling beverage, which cascaded down Cristina's leg and on to the pink dining room carpet.

Cristina's cry of shock and displeasure was of the kind I imagine is seldom heard in such a place. It stopped the proceedings as if a higher entity had hit the pause button - the silence that followed being the kind that fills eternity. Everyone in the room except Seth, who found it all quite amusing, turned their heads away from us while I juggled what was left in the cup and saucer in a hand and forearm that was literally steaming. As the pain subsided, and I managed to regain control, I took on board the realisation that Cristina had gone home to change, taking the skipping child with her. I was alone in a crowded room.

Deciding that I should make some attempt to clear up the mess, I walked toward the kitchen carrying the remains of my coffee. From a distance one of the volunteer helpers leaning on the Aga spotted my approach, and with a word attracted the attention of her co-workers, who immediately stopped their activities, fixing me with their most steely stare, as if defying me to enter their inner sanctum.

Committed to my task, I entered the kitchen, the lever handle of the door slipping neatly up the sleeve of my jacket on the arm that was carrying the cup and saucer which stopped the arm dead.

Unfortunately this wasn't so for the cup and saucer – which continued their journey for quite some considerable distance before crashing to the kitchen floor, at the feet of the now cowering kitchen staff.

Realising that my profuse apologies weren't going to be enough, I returned to the saleroom where the crowd opened before me like the Red Sea before Moses. I purchased a large pink hotel made from clay, that had been someone's souvenir from Mexico, and decided it would probably be for the best if I waited for Cristina outside in the rectory drive.

That day came back to me as I was greeted by Reverend Norwood and invited back into the rectory. We sat in his lounge as I explained the theory concerning time and space. For some reason I felt no sense of nervousness perhaps that was down to the rector's easy manner. We talked for half an hour or more in which time he was in complete agreement with the theory, and even suggested that I met Rosemary Wakelin, the Free Church chaplain at Norwich prison. No, he wasn't suggesting I should be locked up!

The theory of time and space shows how all things in the universe are connected, an idea which is shared, to some extent, with many religions.

Rosemary looks after the needs of all the various denominations incarcerated in the prison. Reverend Norwood thought she would be the ideal person to pass an opinion, so we arranged a meeting. Once again I expounded the theory of time and space, this time feeling even more confident than when I had sat in the rectory and once again it was accepted with enthusiasm.

Rosemary agreed that the Muslims, Christians, Hindus, Jews, Buddhists and the physicists are all united within the glass ball. The sweet woman urged me to let the idea go wherever it would, and I figured that with all things being connected that wouldn't be difficult.

I constantly bounce my ideas off Ray and Wendy, our friends from nearby Blakeney, and one day while taking tea at their house, Ray asked me if I really wanted to test the theory. He went on to explain that in their B&B they had recently had an interesting guest called Karen Sime. Karen is the Personal Assistant to Stephen Hawking. My jaw hit the floor.

Ray suggested that we ask Karen if she would place the theory before Professor Hawking. After a couple of e-mails she agreed, so I edited out the "airy bits" and we sent it to him.

Because of the severity of his illness and the associated communication difficulties Professor Hawking doesn't usually read papers from Joe Public. To me this was understandable, as demands on his precious time must be great, so I didn't really expect anything to come of it. Disbelief turned to euphoria when a few weeks later I received a reply from Karen. She wrote: "Professor Hawking took his time to read through your paper, and then smiled at the end. This indicates that he enjoyed it, although he did not pass comment. Anything he doesn't particularly enjoy is usually signified by a *blank look* or a *grimace,* so you've done very well indeed!"

I take a smile to be positive, as, in this case, does Karen Sime; this then is the theory we sent to the Prof.

I've put the airy bits back in and broken it into simple sections, each of which need be considered and understood before moving on.

TIME AND SPACE

Using man's most powerful telescope astronomers can see 13.7 billion light years out into the universe. Light from those stars has travelled 13.7 billion years to reach us so what in essence we're doing is looking back in time to the birth of our universe.

Everything we see around us, everything in the Universe is made of matter.

When matter is observed through man's most powerful microscope, an inner universe is revealed which is just as fantastic, just as immense as the universe man observes through his telescope. All matter is made of atoms, which are far too small to be observed by the naked eye, measuring about 5 millionths of a millimetre. Now if you imagine that an atom is the size of a football field, then its nucleus would appear smaller than a speck of dust on the centre circle. But the journey doesn't end there. Way down in the nucleus we find strange particles called quarks. There lies the boundary of man's ability to see into that inner space, although many scientists believe that beyond the quark lies another particle which acts as a common link, a unifying field, connecting all things.

Gravity, as anyone who has experienced the pull of Moon on tide will tell you, is a mighty force. It is gravity that keeps everything in its place. The Moon orbiting the Earth, and the Earth orbiting the Sun, and the Sun in its Galaxy, The Milky Way, which in turn has its place in the Universe. The heavier an object, the stronger its field of gravity.

Over 13.7 billion years ago the heaviest area of the universe attracted more and more matter, until ultimately everything had been pulled to that one point. The energy within that place was so awesome that not even light escaped. Once it had sucked everything in, it continued to reduce that matter to a weight so heavy yet small in volume that it goes beyond our imagination. It became the fourth dimension; a place where time and space don't exist. The scientists believe that all the matter in the universe was at this time compressed into a space smaller than the size of an apple.

Try to imagine you are within that place, which incidentally you have to be, as there can be *nothing* outside it. Everything has been reduced to its purest form. Pure, refined energy is all that exists.

Supposing we could be inside that place, observing this perfect unity. There would be no time, as to measure time you need two points of reference, one moving, one fixed, which are constant or reasonably constant like the Earth spinning once in 24 hours, giving us the illusion of our star, the Sun, rising and setting. Likewise with space. To measure a distance, which, again, is a space, you need two points of reference but when there is a complete unity, which is everywhere, there is only one.

Science presently holds itself to be concerned with *the description* of our world. As I touched on earlier, it requires only a moment's thought to realise that a description of unity is logically impossible.

"Description is intrinsically an action that can take place only through the separation of the observer and the observed. This is a barrier which has been recognised in particle physics for many years, and one which is enshrined (if that's the word!) in quantum mechanics."
Fabric of the Universe, Denis Postle.

Now, whether things inside that place just got too dense I don't know, but something triggered a reversal of the process with a bang, which scientists refer to as the Big Bang. In an instant the ball of energy took on three dimensions and began to expand at a phenomenal speed. That was 13.7 billion years ago, and the expansion continues even today, now measuring many billions of light years across. Caught up in this birth of the universe is the expanding ball of pure energy, where nothing has changed. Within this dimension there is still no time or space.

There are still no points of reference in that dimension. It is only in the creation of matter, which was sparked at the moment of the Big Bang, that we have the three-dimensional points of reference required for us to become aware of time and space.

There is no more matter in the universe today than there was 13.7 billion years ago.

Everything we see around us, everything in the Universe is made of matter. Matter is constructed of cells that vibrate at different frequencies. These frequencies are what make us perceive a brick as being hard and an orange soft. At the centre of each of these cells of matter is the dimension of pure energy.

Although science doesn't have the technology which would enable it to see this dimension of pure energy, everything in the natural and scientific world points to its existence.

The unity that existed before the Big Bang still connects everything today, it's just that we now perceive the energy as being rather more spread out, it fills the universe. The energy is now so subtle that we have to be "one" with it in order to access knowledge from it.

How do we become "one with the energy?" Well, we make the ultimate connection when we become totally unfettered by time and space. Unfortunately that's at the point of our death although it is possible to have a foot in both camps. Some achieve this end by meditation, some sing or dance or drum or chant – there are umpteen ways

– but one thing is for certain. Attempting to observe it from outside creates a paradox in which the observer is incompatible, not in harmony and therefore denied access.

Your physical form is linked directly through the generations of your family tree back through history and evolution and beyond right back to the Big Bang. The fact that you made it to here is in itself an impressive achievement. To travel that line from *you* back to the Big Bang would take about 13.7 billion years. On the other hand, the dimension of pure energy connects everything in that line, it is instantly at both places, in the "now" and the Big Bang.

You can only be in one place at a time while confined by the limitations imposed on your physical being by the dimensions of time and space, but on occasions we escape those limitations. The gateway opens as we make the connection through the dimension of pure energy to our past or future self in order to give or receive a helping hand. These connections come to us as feelings of spooky coincidence, divine inspiration, synchronicity, dreams, a ladybird walking up the wall, whatever is available, whatever medium our senses and emotions and intelligence might be able to translate is used to make the connection.

That being the case it stands to reason that our future self has already existed and is handing down the same inter dimensional advice to us to help us become our future self.

This means that death only exists in the dimension of time and space. The instant that death occurs and the restrictions imposed by that dimension are gone, then you become one with the dimension of pure energy which runs through everything including every moment of your whole life, so, therefore, you can return again and again to this life, in fact you never leave it.

What would be the point of returning over and over again?

The point is to learn who and what you are. That you are not a tiny insignificant creature destined to struggle against the angst of this life and die alone - you're much more than that, you exist beyond time and space – you are one with it all.

THE PLANK

It seems to me that when we make a decision on any matter, be it what car we buy or whether or not a plank being used as a bridge across a river will hold our weight, there comes a time, an actual point when we commit, when we make our decision. Now each and every one of us will consider different factors and take a different length of time before making their decision, and for me that's what it comes down to with these scientists who are attempting to prove that everything in the universe is connected.

The scientists agree that everything in the universe points to the fact that a common energy connects everything. It all adds up. They are well aware that the reason they can't actually see it through their microscopes is that our technology is not far enough advanced. They admit that the fact that they are looking for it will distort their findings.

They throw their hands up and cry "until a physics theory is proven it is but a theory of philosophy", but surely when the two are so close that they sit side by side and man is aware that his lack of technology will probably always separate them, then it is time to take a look at the bigger picture.

As human beings we have achieved so much in such a short space of time. Our evolution from apes to where we now stand has been meteoric. But here our evolution has

@♀

ground to a halt. We now appear happy enough to allow the few to manipulate the masses at a catastrophic cost to the planet, when we should be using the knowledge we have acquired for the good of the whole. I wonder how much pain we are willing to inflict on those we oppress in order to sustain our ridiculous lifestyle, how much longer we can continue to lay waste to our planet before the majority can no longer live with a unified conscience that at every turn screams at our senses!

How often do we watch a commercial on T.V., or for that matter the vast majority of the programmes broadcast, finding them a ridiculous insult to our intelligence and put their content down to a subtle marketing ploy by the public relations analyst. The sad truth is that it is not a subtle ploy at all. The content is pure dross! Just because someone is wearing a smart suit and sitting in front of bright lights and cameras, the focus of a multi-million pound industry, we are asked to "believe" that he has something worthwhile to say, that he is telling us the truth, that he has our best interest at heart!

More and more of society now recognises the truth of the seriousness, the depth of the destruction which weaknesses such as greed dictate. The constant, instant access to media coverage shows us how we are directly implicated in the consequences of that greed. The images are irrefutable. So the guys who are in charge of selling us their dross are faced with a tricky conundrum. They realise that society is wising up, but as yet they don't have the strength to make the change themselves. So with self-interest as their driving force and having to combat an ever-increasing loss of trade, their pitch becomes increasingly absurd. Their scams become increasingly obvious as they attempt to scrape the bottom of the barrel for victims.

We see this same scenario in all walks of life. Most of television, Internet, newspapers, the media in general, churning out mind-numbingly futile trivia. How long do we have to tolerate the lie? Well we don't. And the ever growing number of people living in our so-called civilised society who refuse to give power to that lie have found that their lives only change for the better.

There are many different ways in which each and every one of us makes our personal step to freedom, but the giant leap forwards involves one simple question. We all have to answer this question at some stage in our lives and only we ourselves will know when we do.

Using Rule Number 1, (remember Rule Number 1, that we have to find answers within ourselves), using only the evidence which our emotions, senses and intelligence have experienced of such things as feelings of *deja-vu* and synchronicity, of inspiration which touches our heart, or a moment of truth, of impossible coincidences and incredible natural beauty that opened our eyes, or an act of unconditional love which reduced us to tears, or all those moments upon which our life found new direction – from all the intimate evidence of our life experience we have to ask ourselves, do I believe in the unity of all things? Do you believe in the unity, which at this very moment has you reading these words?

THE ROCK

I was very proud of my theory and not just a little excited. I saw it as a material explanation to religion, any religion. No more need for belief in anything other than our own experiences.

Exciting times indeed. To this end I presented my theory to numerous local clergymen and - women, all of whom smiled and nodded their approval – and sent me on my way.

After several such dismissals I began to realise the fact that my theory meant more to me than to them. I'm not sure what I had expected, but judging by my disappointment it was – perhaps – a little more enthusiasm! Eventually I resigned myself to this apathetic reception. After all, in a universe where everything is connected, if something is going to happen, it will, and if my theory was part of that happening, then – what could stop it? Of course I would have to give it a helping hand, that's the way these things work. It's just a matter of recognising the opportunities as they come along.

There is a large piece of blue slate standing in our garden. It is a monument to the realisation of dreams. It weighs about three-quarters of a ton. I know this because I weighed it. I found the rock in a friend's yard in Cumbria. Up there great hunks of the stuff poke out of the ground like great crooked teeth, which the hill farmers are always

@♠

damaging their machinery on. Glad to get rid of these obstacles they dump them in my friend Paul's yard. Paul in turn uses them to form what has the appearance of a giant's rockery in an attempt to stop the ever advancing fell enveloping his house.

We stay at Paul's a couple of times a year, and on one of these visits I admired these great rocks saying that a piece would look good as an ornament in our garden. And so the challenge was issued as he motioned, "take your pick." All I had to do was get it back to *Broadview.*

At the time I was the proud owner of a Ford pick-up which could carry a ton. I planned to drive up and stay over night at Paul's, returning the following day with the rock. Unfortunately the day I planned to return was the day that the petrol strike was scheduled to start. Not to be out-done I decided to do the 500-mile round trip in one day. As I crawled back down the A1, garages were closing as I passed them; others had massive queues snaking out of their forecourts. After a long day, kept awake by Red Bull and Lucozade, in a state of euphoria at having completed the challenge I arrived at *Broadview* along with my wonderful load.

The next day I realised what a problem I was to have in removing the rock from the back of the truck. The chap who does work for us with his digger had no diesel for his machine, or not enough to squander on such a foolhardy scheme, and so the rock stayed on the truck for a few days. When I talked to Paul on the telephone he suggested that I should tie one end of a rope around the pallet which the rock was sitting on, and the other end around a tree.

With this done and the tailgate down I should then drive away as fast as possible.

So that's what I did, and the rock, which I thought would look good in our garden, arrived. I suppose it was a kind of dream. It was something I imagined and I made it happen. There was also a certain element of completing the "macho" challenge to it; such is the bond between my friend and me.

The American in the aisle seat leant over and asked Paul to put out his cigarette. We were in no smoking. Not having flown before, he was uncertain of his position. I backed the American, not that I was well travelled, but I had the understanding that when smoking was permitted it was at the back of the plane, which is what the fog around the rear toilet suggested. For me the absence of ashtrays on our seats clinched it. Still uncertain, Paul agreed with the American that the airhostess should arbitrate.

We were bound for Warsaw in late September 1995 on an adventure. Having now known Paul for over 20 years it is quite obvious that he lives his life as an adventure, although I'm certain he doesn't see it as such.

His wife Jo and he were childhood sweethearts attending the same primary and secondary school in rural Cambridgeshire as Cristina. That's how I got to know him.

Perched on Derwent Fell, just above Keswick, Paul had a yard where he repaired tractors and agricultural machinery and, judging by the way his telephone rang continuously during our stays, he was much in demand. His way of life was hard. The weather usually wet and cold, his working conditions and code of practice saw him taking terrible risks on a daily basis, resulting in a constant update of telephone calls to me, describing how he had crushed, blown up or impaled himself.

Paul had moved to the Lakes more than twenty years ago. He first had a business spreading lime and mowing grass which, once it was established, he sold. Having an affinity with machinery of any kind he got his H.G.V. licence and set up as a repairer of agricultural machinery. He would attend farm sales and auctions up and down the country, buying and selling whatever he could to turn a profit.

It was during this time that he realised the value of the "hay bob". This is a machine that turns the hay after it's been cut and has lain to dry for a few days.

Paul had noticed that the expansion of farms in Holland had made these small machines redundant in favour of much larger models. This meant that he could buy the Dutch machines for virtually scrap value, tart them up and sell them to the hill farmers of Cumbria for a tidy profit. Lovely jubley.

So that's exactly what he did. He would go off to Holland in his massive articulated lorry, a low loader, doing the rounds of farms and auctions buying up hay bobs until, after a couple of years, they began to become scarce. The reason for this was simple, he had literally bought them all. To plug the gaping hole, which now appeared in the market, Paul put into action a plan he had been mulling over for some time. During his visits to Holland he had established that the Dutch company who originally sold the machines had them made under license in Poland. Paul decided to find the source. Enquiries at the Polish embassy revealed that by coincidence there was a large agricultural trade fair taking place in Poznan in a week's time. This was the basis for the adventure that now found me sitting between an amicable American returning to the "old country" and an incorrectly seated chain smoker with a fear of flying.

Arbitrate the airhostess did and in no uncertain terms she pointing out that Paul was indeed in no smoking and that no matter how many times he repeated that he had booked a seat in smoking he didn't have one and wasn't going to get one.

Poland was a friendly place. Even the American, who was met by his cousin, got us a lift to Warsaw train station so we wouldn't get ripped off by the taxi drivers.

Poznan is a pretty University City about 150 miles west of Warsaw where Paul had arranged us B&B through a government agency, who had issued us with a voucher. The voucher carried the B&B's name and address, which was completely beyond the eloquence of our clumsy western tongues, so we showed it to our chosen taxi driver. He studied the piece of paper for some time, the meter ticking away, before nodding his understanding, then proceeded to drive us to the poorer part of the city, its skyline dominated by the sort of stunning Russian architecture you can only appreciate at first hand. Our first impression of the forest of dingy concrete tower blocks that surrounded us was not good.

Ushered out of the taxi, we paid the man, who made no attempt to answer our pleas for further directions, and just like that, we were alone. It was late evening. We stood in the middle of the poor part of a foreign city in a very foreign country clutching a piece of paper, which we couldn't read, under street lights that didn't really work.

All our hopes rested with a youth working in this half-light under the open bonnet of a rusting Lada. As we approached, he straightened from his stooped position, eyeing us up and down, as we rightly deserved. We gestured to him with our piece of paper, asking in perfect English if he could give us directions. He cautiously took it from Paul's outstretched hand, and after regarding it, and us, announced, much to our surprise "you wait". With that he turned, took two bounds and disappeared up the steps into the darkness of the tower block behind him.

As the reality of our situation sunk in, we reasoned that one of three things might happen. Firstly, the youth would return with someone who could give us directions; secondly, he had gone and we would never see him or the piece of paper, the only piece of paper where the name and address of our accommodation was written, ever again; or thirdly he would return with his friends and their baseball bats and rob us. While we thought through the last two scenarios, the first one became a reality with the arrival of another young man who spoke good English and warmly guided us through the warren of concrete pathways to the block we would be staying in. After thanking him, we pressed the buzzer alongside the name Wleklic, that being what was written on the piece of paper. Another young voice, speaking English, this time female and rather excited, greeted our buzzing. Talking through the intercom, she quickly established that we were the expected ones and opened the door automatically from the flat way up above us in the night sky. Such technology impressed me to such an extent that it helped keep me grounded to the fact that I was still just a country boy out on an adventure.

We took the lift to the 10th floor, it always stuck on the 3rd but this could be overcome by pushing the wall of the elevator shaft, which passed by quite openly before us. It seemed to take an age, but when it finally ground to a halt we were greeted by Mrs Wleklic, an elderly widow and her two granddaughters, who shared the flat with her during the week while they attended one of the city's universities. Polish students at that time were given the choice between German and English for their language studies. This accounted for every young person we met having an excellent grasp of English. The girls were no exception and relished the opportunity to put what they had learned to the test. The grandmother used them to interpret her warm welcome as she provided us with all manner of sausages and pickled vegetables. All the neighbours from the 10th floor came to meet us, and everyone was so friendly and helpful that it really did make me feel safe, happy and humble. From the outset it was obvious that these people had very little. The grandmother shared her bedroom with the two teenage girls in order to make some extra money by letting her lounge and spare bedroom. Yet their smiles were genuine and they all made the best of what they had. This was the case everywhere. People with little, being generous and seldom complaining.

The following day we took a tram to the trade fair, accompanied by Agi, a student from Mrs Wleklic's floor. Agi was a pretty 16 year old who had agreed to translate for us as she had no classes that day. She was studying to be a pharmacist and was bright and optimistic about the future, as were all the young people. The vast array of farm machinery did little for me, but Paul was in his element, spending time talking, sometimes with Agi's help, to most of the stallholders, who were eager to make that lucrative contact with the West.

This slow pace continued all morning and well into the afternoon, to the point where I was beginning to get bored. Then Paul spotted and made a direct line for what had brought him on this long journey. It was the company that was manufacturing the hay turning machine. Although sprayed a different colour, they were the same as the redundant machines he had cleared out of Holland. There then followed a lot of nodding and solemn looks as the translation went backward and forward through Agi. Things were written on a scrap of paper and handed to Paul, and after half an hour he had gone as far as he could down this particular avenue.

They would not consider breaking the terms of their manufacturing contract, which prohibited them from selling the machines to anyone outside of Poland. The contract also stopped them from selling more than six machines at a time to any Polish dealer, and on top of that any

Polish farmer buying the machine had to sign an agreement that he would not resell it for three years. When all seemed lost, the salesman, looking furtively from side to side as if checking for eaves-droppers, imparted in hushed tones that of course there were ways round this. And so Paul was given a list of people he should contact who might be able to help him. Because of the language barrier, holding a conversation on the telephone was impossible, but as many of the names on the list were in Poznan, we decided that the best course of action was to visit them, with Agi as interpreter. After doing the rounds of these offices and sales rooms we had found no-one who could help put together a deal, which was looking increasingly dodgy. That said, each person we visited gave him a list of more contacts who might help, and one name kept coming up on every list – a man in Elblag, a city in the North of the country. Paul managed to hold a disjointed telephone conversation with this chap, and was certain that he was the man. The only problem was, we had run out of time. Our visit had been arranged around the trade fair. No one had given much thought to what might happen from there, and we were booked on to a flight home the following day.

That return flight is one that I will never forget. Paul stressed the point that he wanted a seat in smoking, and this time he got one and, like a fool, I got one too - and I don't smoke!

There were six smoking seats, but all the other smokers on the flight would come and stand at the back and light up. The two-hour flight was spent in a smog of the strongest tobacco smoke I have ever breathed. With my eyes streaming and feeling sick, the only consolation was that I had a window seat, so was able to press my face against the glass, where there was a small film of cold air that didn't seem to be as contaminated.

I'm not very good at travelling and holidays, in so far as it takes me weeks to get back into any sort of routine. Not that my life has much of a routine. Maybe that's it; anyway I'd just about got used to being home when Paul phoned to ask if I would like to accompany him to Elblag to meet his shady operative. This time he intended to take the ferry to Holland and drive across Europe. How could I turn down the opportunity of such an adventure? And so it was that a few weeks later, in a £200 Citroen salvaged from a Kendal scrap-yard, we arrived once again in Poznan, where we stayed once again with Mrs Wleklic. We were now into December and the temperature had plummeted to minus 20 degrees. It was so cold that the pre-heater for the Citroen's ignition coil never brought it to temperature. We also had a tyre distort, which made the whole vehicle shake at the cruising speed of 100 m.p.h., apparently the norm for Paul. Changing a tyre in such extreme temperatures isn't fun. And the speed thing, well after the first hundred miles of rigid disbelief, I realised that he wasn't going to slow down, and everybody on the motorway seemed to travel at a similar speed, so eventually I began to relax and resign myself to fate. I would like to add that all the BMWs, Mercedes and Audis cruising along around us were all very expensive, safe-looking vehicles, whereas Paul would tailgate lorries to catch their spray because the Citroen's windshield washer didn't work. When we told the people on the 10th floor that we planned to drive to Elblag the following day they told us we were crazy and Agi refused to come along. The temperature was still minus 20 degrees.

The dock-land setting and Paul's contact could have been out of any gangster movie, and the cold, it was like being in a freezer. At a petrol station we were met by a Pole, who escorted us on foot through a maze of portacabins. We were eventually shown into one of these stark makeshift buildings. Amongst its minimalistic furnishings, in various states of recline, were four men. Worryingly one of them closed the door behind us and remained there. Between the door and us. They fixed us with menacing stares from under thickets of black eyebrows, as though they were imploring us to make one wrong move, which would allow them the excuse to slit our throats and throw our bodies over the quayside. For what seemed an eternity nobody spoke; they drank strong black coffee and smoked strong black cigarettes, and the silence brought home to what extent we were at their mercy. At this point I had given us up as lost and was shaken with relief when Paul pitched in, snapping me out of my melodrama. He was focused on what he had come to Elblag to do, and do it he did. The only man to speak was Paul's contact who, unsurprisingly, had a fair grasp of English. After half an hour the atmosphere in the portacabin had changed; everyone had loosened up, except perhaps me, and Paul's deal was made. Within an hour we were led once more through the maze, and as it grew dark we started the journey down what looked like a river of ice but was in fact the road to Poznan.

The return journey across Europe took three days, due to a blizzard that blocked the E4 motorway faster than the snow-ploughs could clear it. Subsequently we missed our ferry in Holland, and so Paul just kept driving down to Calais.

Over the years I've become accustomed to how relentlessly Paul pursues his dreams, but on that return journey I was continually in awe of his strength, not least of his ability to stay awake. While caught in the blizzard we would be stopped for hours on end, in which time many of the other drivers did fall asleep. When the road ahead was eventually cleared and the slow moving column continued, we would find these stationary sleepers just sitting there in the middle of the road.

A month later the first consignment of ten machines arrived in England.

Such road trips are life changing experiences. I was just along for the ride, but Paul was following a dream, a slightly dodgy dream maybe, but I couldn't help but be impressed by the spirit which drives him to make things happen.

Of course the dreams I am talking about here are the wide-awake wishing dreams. These dreams come true because we make them, but making them come true becomes a whole lot easier when we accept that when we move, the universe moves to help us. Allowing the universe room to make itself known, and being open to make the connection within that space, makes the fulfilment of dreams a lot easier.

Thinking that you are running the show, that you are doing it all on your own, takes away the fluidity and harmony, making progress frustrating and fraught with difficulties which would otherwise have been avoided. The difficulties that arise are after all of our own making. They smother the dream, turning it into another lesson which, yes, does ultimately lead us to the all-important goal but it does so through the experience of wrong turns and dead ends. Understanding which comes through personal experience does create an undeniable form of knowledge, but it's time-consuming and frustrating, and with us humans only having a limited tolerance in these fields, the sooner we learn to work with the universe, the smoother our journey becomes.

THE URGE FOR ADVENTURE

By November 2004 the holiday cottages were earning us a living, and it would be easy enough to just sit back and consolidate our position, which is of course what we were doing. The theory hadn't really advanced very far. I had woven it into a small booklet that I put in the cottages for guests to read. I called it *'The Theory Concerning the Existence of Fairies'*. After all, our guests didn't come to us expecting to be drawn into a philosophical debate concerning the workings of the universe. I reckoned a more direct title with the mention of Her/His Great Omnipotence or the afterlife in might be a bit too scary; maybe I underestimated them.

I had exhibited some of my paintings at the nearby market town of Holt, but in truth I'd only paid for a panel in a gallery and that had cost a fortune. To top it all, my pictures weren't for sale. I told friends that I couldn't bear to let them go, but also deep down there was the fear of rejection.

These were frustrating days, and, as always when faced with things not going my way, the petulant child had a hissy fit and made lots of noise and talked about leaving, maybe finding a place where it would be appreciated.

When your roots go deep it gets hard to pull them up. My family has lived in this immediate area for the past couple of hundred years. It seems unbelievable to me that I've

☻♫☻

been here almost half a century. Time eats away at a lifetime so sneakily that if you aren't watchful, one day it's all gone, and it's too late to do, say and see all those things you'd dreamed of. Things that would have been great things are left undone. While it's comforting to have an immense sense of being part of a place, of belonging to it, there is also an element of familiarity breeding contempt, in that the affinity which serves to comfort also becomes your jailer. I don't wish to sound ungrateful and I realise that I'm extremely fortunate to have been born and be able to remain in a place of such outstanding natural beauty, but sometimes I get the urge for adventures, for leaving, if only for a while.

It was to this end that in the spring of 2003 we bought a VW campervan. Over the previous year we'd made several visits to Brownhills, a large dealer of such vehicles at Newark, each time coming away disillusioned by our lack of funds. We'd wanted a van with a shower and toilet, but they were way beyond what we could afford, and so it was that we found ourselves looking over a VW Trident. A 2-litre petrol engine on a T4 chassis, which had been fitted out by a top-of-the-range converter, called Auto Sleeper. The VW stood out because it was the only one which we could afford, but we agreed that even at its supposedly low price the mileage was too high for a petrol engine. If it had been diesel it would've been OK, but before we could slide the side door closed, the salesman pounced. He did his pitch demonstrating all the equipment and explaining that the bigger vans couldn't get into the places the VW could. "After all", he enthused, "many 4 by 4s have the same dimensions". He even volunteered that the company would touch in the little piece of rust just below the windscreen. He suggested we should take it for a test drive, using salesmanship so subtle it was almost imperceptible. I knew that we were being sucked into making the purchase, but in hushed whispers around the back of the vehicle, Cristina and I agreed that we were both strong enough to withstand him. There was no way we would buy a petrol engine van, but test driving this model might be a good experience in case a diesel version was to become available. So we agreed.

It was at this point that a strange thing happened. The salesman got in the driver's seat, turned the key and there, on the dashboard, lit up in orange, was the ignition coil pre-heater light. The engine was in fact a 2.4 flat diesel and had been incorrectly advertised. There was a pause of a few seconds, which was made to seem much longer by the salesman who silently stared at the wrongly marked sales details, which he had removed from the windscreen and now rested across the steering wheel. Cristina and I talked openly that in fact this was what we had been looking for and were now eager to take the test. The salesman reluctantly left his preoccupation with the obvious implication of the error, presumably by the amount of concern he was giving it the error was quite possibly his, or at least the buck was going to stop with him. And so it was in this pre-occupied state that he drove us out on to the busy dual carriageway where, after a mile or so, he pulled into a lay-by to allow me to take the wheel. I negotiated a round-about, returning towards

Brownhills. Up ahead a delivery van had broken down and was being worked on in a lay-by, which distracted our salesman enough from his thoughts of the possibility of his forthcoming dilemma to comment, "Oops, poor sods." This was quite ironic because, as his words of commiseration were leaving his mouth, the VW's engine suddenly lost power then died, leaving us to coast into the other end of the same lay-by. It was the fuel supply that had also brought about this second hiccup. We had in fact run out of it, and had to make our way back to the dealers on foot along the verge of a very busy dual carriageway, leaving the forlorn VW behind.

Fortunately, the thunder of the continuous flow of heavy traffic made conversation with the salesman impossible. As we trudged along Cristina and I took the opportunity to fall behind and, shouting into each other's ears, confirmed that we both understood the implications of our situation. The fact that we knew we had the right to buy the van at the marked price, were the same thoughts, unless I'm much mistaken, which were occupying the salesman's mind. His almost being flattened by a car transporter as he misjudged his break for the central reservation reinforced this view. That being the case our opportunity to buy would need a swift decision.

After a sweaty, grimy but very thought-provoking walk back to the office, there followed a short silence, then a flurry of openness in which we all put our cards on the table about knowing our rights. The salesman then left us for a further half an hour, returning every few minutes to assure us that he would soon have it sorted.

Finally Brownhills agreed to let us have it at the marked price. Then came the paranoia of "this is too good to be true". I mean, such moments of good fortune so very rarely come my way. Sensing, from the look of scepticism on my face, that the company's loss was not my concern, and in order to impress on me what an honest lot they are at Brownhills, he presented me with the file on the vehicle, which had all their internal documentation. It showed the price they had paid for it from the previous owner, which was the same as their sale price.

Brownhills' man was even good enough to stand by his offer to touch in the little piece of rust below the windscreen.

Every van they sell is given a thorough going over inside and out and is then demonstrated to the customer. The waiting list for this procedure is quite lengthy, and it would be two weeks before we could actually bring the van home. The day before the collection date a chap from Brownhills' body shop telephoned to say that it was more than a spot of rust which he had "just been presented with". His stressing the "just been presented with" was his attempt at deflection of any guilt that might be aimed at him. He told us that to do a proper job he would have to remove the windscreen, and so we would have to wait a little longer before we could pick the camper up.

We considered ourselves fortunate that they were being so thorough, and the new collection day soon arrived. We were shown by the helpful assistant how the fridge, heater, cooker etc worked and, before we knew it, found ourselves sitting outside the gates of their compound. The following journey home, some 100 miles, was fraught with apprehension. Due to the abrupt and premature end to our test drive, we hadn't had the chance to really get a feel for the 2.4 diesel engine but, after having driven it just a mile up the road, it was obviously gutless or had some terrible fault. By the time I'd got to *Broadview,* with Cristina following in our Citroen 1.9 turbo diesel that goes like a rocket, I'd persuaded myself that the lack of power was obviously why the van had been what we perceived as cheap. It seemed that if we were to continue down this avenue of adventure, it would be at the frustratingly sedentary speed of 50 miles an hour.

For two weeks I beat myself up over the purchase of this powerless piece of scrap. Had I learned so little about checking every detail when parting with such large sums of money? In the hope that our local VW centre might be able to shed some light on the problem, we booked it in and dropped it off. Expecting the worst we went into town and did some shopping, returning later in the day to be greeted by a smiling VW rep. He handed me a bill for £15 for test driving the van and then removing the piece of carpet which was jammed under the accelerator pedal, preventing it from travelling any further than half its capable distance. The embarrassment at my stupidity was far outweighed by my relief, which became euphoric as I pulled away from the garage in this wonderful machine with an engine that will pull all day at 70 miles an hour if you ask it to. Of course, you don't, because once you're in the van, on an adventure, nothing, especially speed, really matters. The days just unfold in front of you, while everything you need is there with you. It really does empower you with a great sense of freedom.

Our first trip out took us up to the Lakes. We felt there was safety in visiting old haunts, where we knew the roads and places to park – and Paul was close by, should any catastrophe overtake us. The learning curve is steep when you attempt to live in a space with the floor size of a table tennis table. Having many years of a happy marriage behind us helped, as attempting the most ordinary task demands a most perfectly co-ordinated dance, and as with any such performance, the choreography requires practice, but after a couple of trips we really were getting into the swing of things. Those early days are made easier by the club you join when you own a campervan. You don't sign up or pay any dues, you just sit behind the wheel and drive, and the first van that passes you going the opposite direction will wave to you. Anoraks, we said, but the next van waved, and the next, by which time it was too late, we were in, we began returning the greeting.

There can only be one thing more boring than other people's holiday snaps, and that has to be other people's actual written accounts of their holidays, but that's not what this is about. Just stick with me here. There is a point.

Next we went down to Cornwall to visit the Eden Project and the lost gardens of Heligan. We broke the journey by staying at Longleat, from where we visited Stonehenge, and the Tor and Abbey ruins at Glastonbury. It was magical. Perhaps the energy one feels at the ancient sites is merely due to the magnificence of the structures, but if you apply my theory about time and space, it explains the intensity of that mysterious invisible energy.

In a dimension where time and space do not exist, a dimension where everything is connected, the energy of every soul who has ever stood and marvelled at any particular sacred site is concentrated there, with you. Imagine going to Wembley and watching England play but being the only person in the ground. However much in awe of your surrounding and team you might be, standing alone and shouting "Come on England" in such a situation is going to feel awkward. But now imagine the stadium is full of people singing and cheering; the common love the crowd has for their team unites you and them, creating an euphoric atmosphere. Now imagine you are watching England at Wembley amongst thousands of likeminded people, all cheering for their team, but, other than you, that huge crowd is invisible. This accounts for the spooky feeling of energy we feel at such places.

The vision, dedication and focus required to construct such wonders are immense. With any project, the making of plans, as I mentioned when talking about the renovation of *Broadview,* is the easy part.

The planning of any monumental task requires a period of mental, financial and physical preparation, which is most important. As with all such undertakings, you have to be in the right state of mind if you are to give yourself completely to the task before you. To be preoccupied with any doubts of its success or of one's ability to finish, throws a cloud over the whole proceeding. Paul's plans for the building of the rockery to protect his house had also included the landscaping of his garden and the complete rebuilding of his house. They were big plans and so they took a lot of preparation. It actually took four years' mental preparation before the reconstruction work finally began.

Paul had bought a massive tracked digger and two dumpers, that he was using to rebuild the side of the fell and landscape around his house. He also had a steady supply of rocks varying in weight from about a quarter of a ton up to roughly three tons that were being delivered for free to his yard by the local water authority. They were digging a pipeline route near his house and glad to get rid of them. A few years earlier I had been impressed enough with these massive stones to have carted one 250 miles on the back of a clapped-out Ford pick-up, and now there was this seemingly endless supply available.

Here was an opportunity to make money from nothing! The part of my brain which has a couple of dodgy connections clicked open, flooding out any rational protests from the saner sections of the old grey matter. My instincts should have killed it there and then, as they have at their disposal any number of examples of weird and wonderful money making schemes that over the years have been pursued at great cost and with little or no success. The money-making plan involved selling pieces of stone in local garden centres, a plan requiring several skills, none of which I had. This frustrating formula of seeing an opportunity but not having the where-with-all to fulfil it, has dogged all my weird and wonderfuls. When such potentially golden opportunities pass before me, I become consumed by them; after all, on every trip I make to the garden centres, I smugly search out their pathetic selections of pieces of granite and blue slate, unceremoniously displayed in tubs of sand. Laughingly labelled "monoliths", of which none weigh more than a half a hundredweight, they generally sport price tags of £30 and up. By this measure my three quarter ton rock would be worth almost £1000 – and Paul had an endless supply being dumped in his yard for free. Perhaps you can understand the temptation.

I talked to Paul about the idea, and he agreed that if I could find buyers down South he would arrange the supply of rocks. So, armed with a photo of our rock, I went to the local garden centre and asked the owner whether he thought he could sell such things. He agreed to act as middle man, saying that if we wanted to display some in his car park from which to take orders, then that would be fine, but he wanted no part in the delivery or siting of the pieces. So it seemed that it might be a viable proposition. Then comes the cooling off period where reality kicks in and sanity has just enough time to slam the door in my head shut in order to put across its case.

It's the sheer size of the rocks at Stonehenge, the monumental effort it took to build the Tor and Abbey at Glastonbury. It was the immensity of the domes of the Eden Project, it is the grand scale that they all have in common, and that's what makes them all extraordinary. I figured that to be "extraordinary", the supplied rocks for the gardens would have to be big rocks, massive three-ton obelisks. The bigger the rock, the more impressive it would look – but this was the problem. Once the obelisk went over the size which one man could comfortably handle in a wheelbarrow, the job would involve diggers and dumpers. Now, they tend to make a bit of a mess of your lawns and herbaceous borders, unless the operation is performed with the experience and dedication which comes from "a calling."

The problem with my idea was that I had no experience of using the heavy lifting machines essential in such work. There was always the possibility of sub-contracting, but while I have an interest in the powerful presence of spirit which I sense at such large stone circles, the thought of selling and erecting them held no fascination for me whatsoever. That being the case, I knew the idea was dead in the water; however the idea to do things on a grand scale stuck with me, but then it always has.

The building of *Broadview* was a big scheme. It was my dream to build it, but without our families' help and my father's knowledge of the building trade, it would have been beyond us.

My father, George the builder, loved to build things. All his working life, come rain or shine, he would be on site at 7.30 a.m. until 5.00 p.m. Such a lifetime of hard manual work would have crippled a lesser man. He was always thinking of ways around problems, seeming to effortlessly model piles of flint and brick into beautiful structures. There must be almost a hundred houses in the surrounding villages that he's built.

Father's ties with *Broadview* went back to when he was 13 and had just left school. Not wishing to follow his father and grandfather into the building trade, he decided he would become a gardener. At that time *Broadview* and next-door *Bones Cottage* had been rented to two chaps who had been wounded in the First World War. The cottages came with a couple of acres at the back that were used as smallholdings so as to provide the tenants with an income. After a week or so double digging at *Broadview* father had had enough and asked a couple of brickies he passed on his way home if they had a job for him. And so it was he fell in with the rest of the Balding line. For this reason father's connection with *Broadview* was stronger than mine. For me it was a means to an end, for father it was a step back into his past. That's not to say I didn't have a dream for the building of *Broadview*, it's just that it was different from father's.

We worked together doing the labouring and the building, but it was father who pushed me on, kept me going, keeping to his relentless hours, using his knowledge of traditional methods to save money.

Prompted by father's ideal of seeing the Balding name on the door of a transit truck, I had made a couple of attempts at being a proper builder. We bought property or land and developed it, purely with the idea of making money, but always with disastrous results, each project making little profit for years of back breaking work.

Father loved to build. It was his life and he lived it so ferociously that at times I was frightened of letting him down; I on the other hand built *Broadview* as a means to an end, that end being my interest in the unity that connects all things. I wanted a place where people could come to stay and exchange ideas and tell me about all the different lives they inhabit. My interest was in finding understanding.

When *Broadview* and her holiday accommodation were complete and earning us a living, it was as if a great weight had been lifted from me. The relief was not from the easing of the constant regime of hard manual work, although the onset of arthritis in my wrists and ankles was becoming an annoyance, but more the fact that at last I had free time.

So much free time that at first I could scarcely believe the opportunity that lay before me. The door was open for me to pursue *my* dream.

I initially entered this place like a cat that has lived all its life in a London flat, and then its owner takes it to live deep in the Norfolk countryside. These first steps were introverted and small. Head down, keeping close to the ground. Then came my painting and writing, which the holidaymakers seemed to like. Their encouragement reinforced my self-confidence, my belief that my dream is as good as anybody else's.

For me, a repressed child of the 50s, this public airing of my thoughts was far more daunting than a 21st Century gay stepping out of the closet! As I took those first uncertain steps, I fronted it as best as I could, although inside I was petrified. I held my breath – but nobody laughed or pointed, or if they did, I didn't notice or for that matter care. After all, for years I had told myself and others too, that worrying about what other people think of you stops you from being *you.*

The encouragement of all those people who were sharing my dream pushed me on like a snowball gathering in size and speed, a snowball which, oblivious to consequence, aspired to be an avalanche. This new found confidence, this liberation issued me the challenge to do something big with my dream. After all, it had led me to a fantastic place, so why not share that place with as many people as possible and how better than in a proper book?

As always, such big ideas require large amounts of effort, which at first is just too scary. It's much easier to sit back and hide, to whinge and moan and point the finger at all the wrongs in the world. The problem is that as the pressure builds, you can only keep that position for a little while – then you blow your top!

LETTING OFF STEAM

A good friend is always remarking how I am one of those people who constantly need my ego to be massaged. Well – to a certain extent that is true, but from inside Vaughn, from inside here, it's different. In that place where the voice of my mind mulls over its reasons before turning them to actions, it's more like "I need positive feedback for reassurance and energy, and if I don t believe in myself then I'm done for". I realise that I am just an ordinary chap. I can live with that, but taking that into account, there must be hundreds of thousands of people who are initiating their version of my unifying field theory. After all they will have thought of it just the same as I did.

But if that were the case, things in the world that surrounds us would have begun to change – and I'm not certain that they have.

Looking around the shops in the crowded mall I realised just what a pointless, destructive existence we lead. We have indeed taken the planet right to the brink, right to the edge of the abyss. I had chauffeured Cristina and Emily on a shopping expedition to the city.

The Sky TV playing on the monitor in the coffee shop was telling me that Shell had over-estimated their oil reserves and Prime Minister Blair was cosying up to Libya's Qadhafi (for his oil), and we were in a bloodbath in Iraq (for their oil). This was followed by the sports news with

details of the European cup semi-final. This would be played the following day between Monaco, a tiny principali-
ty where one in eight of the population are millionaires,
and Chelsea, a club which had recently been bought like a
toy by a Russian billionaire. This chap has made so much
money from the production of oil that he can buy whatever his heart desires. That's when I had the dream about
the ancient Chinaman.

This was a proper dream, I mean one of the ones which
comes when you're asleep. No, not in the coffee shop, it
was in the early hours of the following day.

It was quite short or at least it seemed that way. My sleep
had been troubled, which is not unusual for me.
Sometimes I seem to spend all night on the edge of sleep
where thoughts of the waking world cross over into the
strange place of dreams. And that's where I met him, the
Chinaman. Small of stature and dressed in a simple robe,
he held out his hands for me to go to him, which I did. He
hugged me, and as I embraced him I was touched by a
sense of great euphoria, a strange sensation as though
through him he was allowing me to feel his connection to
the very universe itself. The form that he took, the skin
and bones, only represented a physical object. The
Chinaman was indeed more than that. His softly spoken
words filled me, purposely calming me so that I might
remember them. He said, "You must suffer many terrible
deaths but when you have, when you understand them you
will be eternal, you will not have to die again." I instinctI-
vely knew that what he was telling me could be nothing
other than the truth. Then I was back.

Over the next few days I pondered over the deaths the Chinaman had referred to. Perhaps he meant the psychological deaths that occur when we embrace understanding about ourselves. Such understanding requires growth, and growth means change. Letting go of the old and coming to terms with the new, putting aside deeply entrenched opinions and ways, many of which have been etched into our personalities over a lifetime. These changes are all deaths, some trivial, some so immense we feel we can never accept them, though accept them we must, for the alternative is to remain stuck in that part of our development in a state of perpetual mourning. If I was right, then it was spooky, he was backing up my theory.

Sitting in the coffee shop and watching the shoppers come and go, I got to thinking about our craving for the material possessions, which we deem so very vital to our existence that we are destroying the planet on which we live. The irony is that we don't actually need any of them. The need, the want, the urgency to have is created for us by the propaganda machines. They accustom us, the masses, to becoming dependant on their products and so we work to earn money to buy them. This chain of work and payment, deals for profit, directly links whole nations with self-centred lifestyles to the exploitation of whole nations forced to survive on next to nothing. When the disadvantaged sense of loss is mixed with the euphoria of a religion it creates a heady mixture that is so easily sparked into war or terrorism but religious fervour is only their excuse for war, what is really being fought for is material possessions.

Please don't get the wrong end of the stick here; I believe it to be the God-given right of any people oppressed by greed to rebel against it, but not to do so in the name of religion. To suggest that empowers their oppressor with the excuse that he is also fighting a holy war. What a ridiculous phrase, holy war.

The root of any true religion is love and peace and should never be mistaken for the corrupted versions sold to us in the name of the war-mongers of capitalist greed or the extremist militants who use rhetoric to ignite the disadvantaged desperate cry for freedom.

Oil is the most valued commodity of our 21st Century lives. It powers the material world that we are all so dependent on. Without it everything would stop immediately.

Growing fears now come not so much from indications that the oil might be running out but rather that time is.

The effects of global warming become more evident with each natural disaster that strikes. Unfortunately it's only when such catastrophes begin to effect us personally that we tend to take note.

A time when we all move to the use of natural energy like solar, wind and tide, has to be a good thing. Sadly the window in which we can make the transition is becoming very small. Scientists now predict that if decisive action isn't taken to restore the planet's eco-system within the next 15 years (date of writing 05-05-04) the damage will be irreversible. This in effect is a prediction for the extinction of the human race.

The changes should have been implemented 30 years ago, when the scientists first issued their warnings. After all, we knew the oil wouldn't last forever. Surely it would have been prudent to perfect alternative methods of energy production. Perhaps this new technology already exists, but in these days when new ideas are only released when their predecessor has been milked for every penny, means we will be using oil and fossil fuels until the cost to the people and the planet becomes unacceptable.

Meddling with a force greater than oneself is always very dangerous, so might I suggest that unless we take drastic action towards implementing changes that redress the natural balance ourselves – now! – then a greater power will step in.

Have you ever wondered that in a total solar eclipse the moon is at precisely the right distance between the Earth and the Sun to fit exactly, causing the eclipse, and creating that wonderful diamond ring effect as it reappears? That's natural balance. The beating of a hummingbird's heart, the colours of the rainbow, the pull of moon on tide, the trail of the shooting star – these wonders demonstrate the power, precision and symmetry which nature effortlessly creates.

If man will not redress the balance, then nature will.

So, time and oil are running out. I would like to say "Thank God for that" but I'm afraid it might be misconstrued as a leaning towards one particular religious belief, which, incidentally, I don't have. Mother always said that a person's religion can be seen in the way they live their life – no matter what religion they *say* they are. I've never really thought much about religion beyond that, but it does seem to have been hijacked and used as a way of dividing and controlling people. The sad thing is that the initial idea at the root of the major religions has as its basis the tenet that love for your fellow man is the way, which in my mind is spot on.

That being the case, how did Islam, Judaism and Christianity, become so divided, especially when they are easily traced back to a point in time where they all worshipped the same God.

Sadly, you don't have to look very deeply to find this information. This in itself says something about the way we blindly except what is happening in the world. It's easier not to ask the questions.

It begins some 4000 years ago with Abraham having two sons by different wives. The lineage of these two sons becomes Islam and Judaism. Each branch of Abraham's family claim to be the "chosen" line and each believe their man to have been the "favourite" son. So these two arguing children, both arrogantly believing themselves to be better than the rest of his family, choose to fight one another over a story written 4000 years ago! To ask us to seriously believe that centuries of revenge and reprisal rest on such a foundation is an insult to man's intelligence, an embarrassment to the planet. Indeed if they were children they would both get their ears tweaked and be told to grow up.

When you take a nation of oppressed people and mix them up with rhetoric, it is easy to incite a crusade at the root of which will always be found the desire for material possessions. Those material things might be those which we as a nation view as our basic rights such as food and water or a roof over our head, in a place where we don't have to live in fear. Then again it might be oil or gold or land, but it certainly isn't religion.

Oh and the Christians! Where do they come into it? Well, it appears that the Christians split from Judaism when Christ came on the scene. This is the story of the New Testament, that tells us the son of God, Jesus Christ, was crucified at the behest of the Jews, who wanted to crush the new cult. This appears to have been the excuse used for anti-Semitism over the following 2000 years. But consider this; when the armies of one country forcibly occupy another for any length of time, it is they who have the privilege of being the ones who record their version of events. They write the history.

At the time of the Roman occupation of Palestine, rebellion was spreading like wildfire. Feeling their grip on power being threatened, the Romans took out the rebel leaders, and over the next 300 years, seeing that they weren't going to beat this one with force, and being the cunning tacticians that they were, they coined the phrase "if you can't beat 'em, join 'em" and got themselves religion.

So as to keep themselves out of the mire for the killing of the leader of their newly adopted faith, they used the Apostle Paul's version of events, in which Pontius Pilate had really been quite a nice guy who didn't want Christ killed. The Apostle Paul had been a citizen of Rome, and Pontius Pilate had in actual fact been a butcher who crucified Christians by the thousand. This is not to say that the moral message in the Roman version of things isn't spot on. I marvel at how so much survives intact through the numerous translations it's suffered over the years, but few could argue with the fact that the book was written with a slant towards the authors. I mean, think about it. A brutal army of occupation trying to subvert the vibrant eloquent rebel leader of the 'good' guys, and there's not a mention of them being the bad guys. I'm afraid that side of the book smacks of Papist propaganda, which is fine unless you are one of the millions of Jews who have since been persecuted for being falsely put in the frame!

So that's my take on religion, politics and capitalism.

What's my reason for talking of such things? Simply the massive discrepancies between what we are told, or at least asked to believe, and what "is", what we see with our own eyes. When we have reached such an obvious point of contradiction then the only way reason can unravel the puzzle is to think outside the box.

ABSENT FRIENDS

In early September 2004 a friend of ours went into hospital, he was losing his sense of balance. They suspected it might be a problem with his inner-ear. It turned out to be a brain tumour. Three months later only the drugs being used for his pain management were keeping him alive. It was hard to watch. The occasions on which he surfaced, from the place between life and death, where he drifted, became fewer and fewer, until, at last, he was gone.

Peter and his wife Carol, both civil servants, had retired from their profession when their son Luke was born, which was also the same year that our daughter Emily came into the world. The smallness of our community made it inevitable that through the shared territory of child rearing our paths would become intertwined, and so it was that we became friends.

Peter was an atheist and a dreamer, quite the opposite of Carol. The sad thing on the dreaming side was that some dreams never got beyond the 'buying-of-the-equipment-required-to-put-them-into-action' stage. Over the years their garden had become a graveyard of these unfinished projects. Abandoned boats, caravans and vintage cars, all in various states of repair, all covered in varying degrees of green algae, which marked the point when interest had faltered and inevitably moved on. Peter's garages had filled with all manner of machinery that would be used to build all manner of inventions. His office was strewn with the plans for fun-fair rides and road trips and fabulous eco-friendly houses that he would one day build. Likewise his head was full of far away places that he was going to visit. And so it was that about a year previous to his illness, we took it with a pinch of salt when Peter announced that he and his family were going to fly around the world, stopping off at just about everywhere en route.

For anyone else this would indeed be an attainable dream, but there was a problem. Carol suffered from a serious fear of flying. Whenever they visited their friends on the continent, they always took the ferry, but now tired of the confines dictated by Carol's phobia, Peter was throwing down the gauntlet. He issued the challenge that she either conquered her fear and flew with them, or stayed at home on this particular trip. Peter had gone so far as to get the details of a course run by the local airport that was tailored to help would-be flyers conquer such nervous dispositions. Carol would have none of it, and so it was that we watched with a sense of "good for you mate" as he and Luke flew off on their adventure.

It wasn't that he had stood up to Carol, that's not what this is about. Anyone who had spent any time with them would tell you it was obvious that they were devoted to one another. No, the thing that impressed us was the fact that Peter had stood up to himself. He had let himself fulfil a dream.

Such was our admiration of our friend that Wendy made Ray and me t-shirts that proclaimed across the front

"Peter Bryant is our hero". Upon his return we thought it best to wait for a time when we could catch him on his own. The chance came and we went around to hear about his adventures.

We wore sweatshirts over the T's with the idea that after a while Peter would go into the kitchen to make us coffee, and when he returned into the lounge – "Surprise"! Something so simple, what could possibly go wrong?

Ray was closer to Peter than I was, and watching the disease take his friend was hard for him. At one stage of his despair he remarked to me that he felt Peter had nothing left. His garden was full of unfinished dreams, the doctors had given him no hope and – he was an atheist. He didn't believe in anything, no god just dust to dust.

At the time, with my thoughts focused on our friend's demise, the implications of this remark didn't seem important, but as the days went by, it kept coming back to me.

It seems to me that atheists choose to rely on their kno-wledge and life experiences to form their own opinion of life and death, rather than blind belief. They believe in the material world that they experience at first hand through their senses – which is exactly what my theory demonstrates.

Up until then I had been printing my booklets on my com-puter under the title *'The theory concerning the existence of fairies'* which I chose for its mysterious, esoteric yet safe feel. Now, in the clinically hard, cold, white light of day that comes with the death of someone close, I felt that the time for skirting around the issue was gone. I decided to address it head on with a more in-depth book revealing the hard truths omitted from *'The theory concerning the existence of fairies'*.

I realise that my new hard-line might be thought contentious by some advocates of the "New Age" shops that sprang up in the 90's selling crystals, tarot cards, spells and charms. The White Witch proprietors of such establishments, and their connection to Mother Earth, provide a much needed gentle introduction to a mysterious esoteric world; unfortunately, upon leaving such shops, and faced with life and all it's tragedies, the magic, woven with incense and calming music, can all too quickly weaken and come undone.

Given time to think, I began to realise a cold truth about Ray's atheist remark.

Ray runs a B&B with his wife Wendy, prior to which Ray had been in teaching; a headmaster who went on to teach teachers. He opted out of the rat race in one of those spur-of-the-moment decisions on which lives pivot and change direction. One day in the middle of a lesson he took the clock off the classroom wall, closed his briefcase, and went home, where he made a large bonfire from all his work-related files. He never looked back, and moved to Blakeney to run his B&B where said clock hangs in his kitchen – where time is his own. Over the years Ray has become a friend whose opinions I value greatly. I constantly use him to sound out my ideas, especially my theory concerning our existence in other dimensions. It was, after all, he who helped me get it put before Professor Hawking; and so every time I updated my "hand-made on the computer" booklet, I've given him a copy.

When asked for a critical opinion he has always maintained that we share many similarities in our opinion of the unity of all things, he's such a diplomat, but that's OK, the theory is a bit tricky and eventually everybody 'gets it', it's just that we don't all get it at the same time. It's only the outline of the theory that can ever be explained. The core of the understanding has to come from within.

Do you remember those pictures that were very fashionable towards the end of the 90s? I believe they were called Magic Eye pictures. They consisted of what appeared to be an abstracted swirl of coloured dots, but as you concentrated on the picture and allowed your eyes to drift out of focus, an obvious shape would appear.

My parents, who are in their 80s, thought they were amusing, so did Cristina and the children. For a few moments they would go zombie-like before grinning widely and exclaiming "it's a dog on a surfboard", or "a cow jumping over the moon". They and all our friends loved them, but do you think I was ever blessed with the sight! It was most frustrating – but imagine that the roles were reversed and that you can see a wonderful four-dimensional picture – which nobody else can, now wouldn't that be really frustrating!

At first you might begin to doubt your sanity, but gradually reassurance, in the form of company, comes to comfort you, showing you that you're not alone, in fact quite the contrary. You are part of an ever-growing multitude of people who are beginning to sense the 4th dimension. All in varying degrees and all from their point of view.

There will always be those of us whose combination of curiosity and loose tongue will give rise to the urge to 'get loud' about their passion, but we're all different, so, please, try not to take exception as the fire and brimstone evangelists implore: "You gotta lay your burden down in order to approach the theory. Free yourself of your mental hang-ups and you'll fall naked into it, becoming one with the very universe itself. Coming to realise who and what you are starts you tumbling, but until you've passed the point of no return there is always a tendency to draw back, and with such doubt there always follows ineffectiveness". Actually, the last bit was probably Goethe.

Serious thoughts, prompted by the finality of Peter's illness, had me thinking that it would only be right to fill you in on a few of this book's background details. Just little things like the story about Mr. and Mrs. Christmas.

After writing the story, I e-mailed it to them for their approval. The reply came swift and straight to the point, the point being that they weren't in fact married – least ways not to each other!

They had partners and were fathers and mothers of children in those marriages. They had other lives. Mrs Christmas explained how they had been in love for a long time and that they were both trapped in their unhappy marriages, but couldn't break up the family unit for the sake of the children. She implored me that, if I used the story, I would change names and places; which, of course, I did.

Upon reading this revelation, I thought I wouldn't be able to use the story; but then, after mulling it over and applying Rule Number 1, – You remember Rule Number 1? That you don't try and figure out why other people are like they are or why they do the things they do; in essence, you don't judge anyone other than yourself. With Rule Number 1 applied all that remained was the initial positive feelings that were evoked when we met the couple – which was after all what made me write the story in the first place.

Standing in the lounge waiting for Peter to return with the coffee, Ray and I removed our sweatshirts to reveal our "Peter Bryant is our hero" t-shirts. There then followed an awkward wait, during which I suddenly became very self-conscious and began to question our being there. The sound of Peter approaching indicated that it was too late to reconsider and we both went into a stance preparing for him to walk through the door. At roughly the same instant Ray and I realised that the reason we could hear Peter approaching was that he wasn't alone; he was talking to Carol – who now entered the room to be greeted by dumb and dumber. Such embarrassment isn't easily explained away – although I left Ray to try.

One of our four cats, Woody, died this morning. 28 November 2004. She had been ill for a few months, her life noticeably draining away. She gave up the ghost on the same spot, in the kitchen, where she had entered *Broadview* some 10 years earlier. A short life by some measures of cat life, and probably not really a very happy life by the measure of bad experiences. Firstly she was from a cats' home. Taken from her mother quite early, she was a sickly kitten for the first few weeks that we had her, but eventually she came good. After a couple of years, which thinking back must have been the happiest of her life, she had a litter of kittens. During a scorching Wimbledon afternoon it became obvious that the cat was having difficulty delivering them herself, so we took her to the vet, who assured us, grim-faced, that the then unborn kittens were all dead and that a caesarean was necessary if we were to save the mother. We could pick her up the following day.

That night we had tickets to see Kirsty MacColl in Norwich. On returning from the concert we received a message from the vet, asking us to go to the practice and pick up Woody and the kittens – immediately. The vet had been wrong; the kittens had all survived, but as Woody had given birth under general anaesthetic, she didn't recognise them as her own, so subsequently refused to feed them. He suggested that we take them home and try to wean them ourselves.

Over the course of several heartbreaking days and nights I attempted to feed the kittens with a syringe. This was the vet's idea and, as I found out later, was not the most effective method of hand weaning! In fact it didn't work at all! Needless to say the kittens died one by one, until there was only the largest of the litter left. I had a brainwave and phoned the cat sanctuary, looking for a surrogate mother and was in luck. A cat had given birth to a litter a couple of days earlier and had lost a kitten, so there was a chance that she might take ours. I rushed over to the cattery with the last kitten, which the surrogate happily took. What joy!

It lasted about 12 weeks – the joy.

We were summoned to the cattery to pick up the kitten, which we named Kirsty. As with Woody, Cristina and I both thought it was too young to have been taken from its new mum, and after two days of eating and drinking practically nothing, Kirsty had a fit. Dissatisfied with the veterinary attention we'd received at the kitten's birth, we took the poor creature to a different practice. They put her to sleep immediately.

Woody remained completely indifferent, but the whole process knocked me back. I'd got it into my head that I was going to keep that kitten alive – but I couldn' t.

Woody's life just got worse from then on. We all understood that she wasn't responsible for her inability to mother the kittens, but I think we all felt differently about her. Emily, who was 7, was distraught over the deaths and so as to lift her spirits, we allowed her to get a new kitten of her own, which she called Velvet, and to lift our spirits at the same time we got our puppy, Phoebe.

We thought Woody would be alright with the two new arrivals. We hoped that from the outset, being bigger and more aggressive, she would establish her position as the boss, but she decided to do just the opposite, having nothing to do with them – and moved into the garden shed.

And that's where she lived out the remainder of her life, avoiding Phoebe and Velvet – almost feral.

Towards the end she came back into the house, too ill to care, which the other animals sensed and respected, finally leaving her be.

It's only a cat, the cat-haters will say, but I'd grown attached, the way some people do, and I felt I'd let her down. I'd chosen her from the cattery and then brought Phoebe and Velvet to *Broadview,* and they'd chased her out.

I buried her under the blue cedar, where a few years earlier I'd buried her kittens, marking the spot with a heavy concrete slab and a birdbath.

Peter's illness lasted about three months, the numbing reality that he wasn't going to escape death only making itself known in the final four weeks. At first Ray put his hope in the power of positive thought and then a macrobiotic diet, which his fitness coach had suggested, but as the prognoses became ever more desperate, so were the straws that were grasped at.

Prompted by his love for Peter, and without Peter's knowledge, Ray instructed a faith healer who lived in France – Ray would try anything if it might save his friend.

Peter was dignified, quite content in his belief – the concern tending to rest more with those closest to him. Such was the sense of their loss.

After we'd had the camper van for a couple of years, a few spots of rust started to appear along the bottom edges of the vehicle. I took it to the chap who does our bodywork. He told me in a pointed tone that the van had undergone a complete re-spray; and you don't re-spray a vehicle unless you have a problem with rust! Not a bargain after all!

Peter Bryant. 28 December 1946 to 8 December 2004.

THE ROCK
(Continued)

Getting the rock from Cumbria to *Broadview* wasn't the end of the story. It now had to be moved about 10 yards and placed upright on a concrete slab, which I'd put down in preparation. The rock is about 40 inches high with a shape not unlike Mount Everest. Fortunately, due to the way slate forms, it cracks along seams, and my Everest had a flat bottom. This made the up-righting part of the job relatively simple, it would just require some concerted levering with some scaffold poles. It was the moving of the three-quarter ton weight that was going to require some thought.

The site we had chosen for the rock was in the grounds surrounding two of the holiday cottages, where we had in residence two couples.

Each couple were strangers to the other, they were made more interesting to me by the total oppositeness of their characters.

Charlie and Pat were very quiet, deep thinking, country folk, who made their living from running their own game shoot. Sharon and Billy on the other hand were bubbly and game for a laugh, enjoying a lively social life.

The commotion created as Seth and I assembled the jacks, scaffold poles, boards and all the associated paraphernalia

●♀☺

required for the task aroused the interest of these two couples, and before long both men came over to investigate – shortly followed by their wives.

Over the next couple of hours the six of us devised a plan and put it into action, the end result being the rock coming to its final resting-place, upright on the slab.

Sharon opened another bottle of wine and we all toasted our achievement, and not wanting the party atmosphere to end, the guests all decided that that very night they would go out for a meal together. The rest of the week they became good friends, and before they left, they booked the same weeks for the following year, so that they could meet up again. This went on for several years. In between times they would come down for their birthdays, kindly inviting us along to join in.

They say that opposites attract, and I guess that's what was happening here. But such attraction requires compromise by both camps in order to bring them closer together. If not, it's simply a case of the satisfaction of curiosity.

The last occasion when they all stayed was a birthday jaunt. We all went round to the local, the *Wiveton Bell,* for a meal. As we enjoyed the hospitality Sharon, quite suddenly, appeared to become the worse for drink. This was early evening, and by 9 p.m. she required carrying to the car. She passed out about an hour later during coffee in *'March Hare'.*

The following day it was explained that when Sharon was younger, a horse had rolled on her in a riding accident, fracturing her skull, which led to these incidents occurring on occasions.

The two couples came to Broadview to take a glimpse into each other's worlds, and then they were gone.

The rock, however, remains – along with its story, which still hasn't fully been told.

You see, as I told you earlier, the rock was one of many that had been dumped in my friend Paul's yard, in order for him to build a giant rockery. The only thing was that the particular farmer who was dumping the rocks in Paul's yard wasn't doing it out of friendship, least ways not for the friendship of Paul.

It had always been a struggle for Paul, making a living repairing farm machinery. It wasn't that he couldn't do his job, because there was no one better, but rather it was his easy going nature which let him down, in so far as he was sometimes taken advantage of. The hill farmers of Cumbria are renowned for their loathing for parting with money, which meant long hours, and appalling working conditions for little remuneration.

In an attempt to ease the situation, he had been drawn into a scheme instigated by one of these very farmers. Barry Hook was a local entrepreneur who needed just such a hard working chap with a H.G.V. licence to help him collect farm machinery from all over Europe, which was then exported to the American mid-west. These foraging expeditions kept Paul even busier and seemingly no better off, and now thousands of miles from home.

In spite of having lived in the Lakes for almost 20 years, Paul and Jo would always be considered outsiders by the tight-knit farming community, who they thought to be their friends. However, they had recently been allowed into a circle of about six or seven of these truly local couples, who met up regularly for meals and barbecues, even holidays. On one of our visits we were invited along to one of their get-togethers, a murder mystery meal, where, as you ate, a plot unravelled, culminating in cheese and biscuits with one of the company being unmasked as the perpetrator of the dastardly deed.

The only people who knew the plot and therefore the identity of the murderer were the host and the murderer, who, coincidentally, just happened to be sitting next to me and opposite Jo.

Cristina decided not to attend what would turn out to be a surreal evening's entertainment, opting to baby-sit Paul and Jo's children.

The drama was to be played out in costume so we all spent an amusing day going around the charity shops of Kendal looking for outfits. I was to be a photographer accompanying a hack journalist who would be played by Paul. Mine was one of a few roles created for the unexpected guest, allowing them to take part as an observer and not disturb the already laid out plot. I found a long cream coat, hat and camera, which I thought looked the part. Paul, almost in the first shop, came across a gaudy chequered suit that was spot on. Jo – well, I can't quite recall the character she was to play, but it obviously required a crimson ball gown which took a long while to find, and was cut so low it left little to the imagination.

When we arrived, the rest of the guests were kitted out in 1920s evening wear, and we all looked pretty authentic, even if I say so myself. The meal got under way, and the plot slowly unravelled along with its multitude of red herrings, but it always had the feel that another plot was being played out and, moreover, this sub-plot was one which was known by all the guests seated around that table – except Paul and me.

Subsequently, a week or so after our return to Norfolk, Paul phoned in a terrible state to tell me about the affair.

Jo couldn't explain why she had done it and promised she never would again, and pleaded for forgiveness.

Paul shouted and raved and hid in a bottle for months. When he came out he had with him the conclusion that he had excluded Jo from his world, even though it was a world in which he struggled to make them a living and pay the mortgage etc, and for that reason he was partly to blame. He decided that he didn't want to start over again with another woman, so instead he and Jo would begin their lives together once again. Things could never be the same. However, he had decided on a course of action, which he blustered over from time to time, but which, as the months and years roll by, can be seen as the most wonderful act of forgiveness.

But what of the perpetrators of the real crime – the community, which they thought they were becoming part of. It had used them both and spat them out: Jo for their amusement, and Paul as their lackey.

For starters Paul and Jo agreed not to hide what had happened to them. The farmer's wife, without further ado, was told of her husband's indiscretion. Paul then began his vendetta. Every secret that over the years the farming community had poured out to him as he slaved over their mechanical problems, little snippets of information given out like accolades as if to show their trust and friendship – in the hope of deferring payment; all these snippets had been carefully filed in Paul's head and were now called forward piece by piece, usually at the bar of the local. Matter of factly dropped into conversation setting neighbour against neighbour, tarnishing friendships and stirring up that oh so cosy, little, set in its ways farming community.

Paul now cut himself off from that community. Whenever we had visited previously, the phone had rung continually and people he had called friends sat around his large kitchen table drinking his coffee. Now there was nothing, few of them rang or called. They knew that they were no longer welcome, and that they should stay away.

Paul would repair no more of their clapped-out machinery, nursing them along with favours; he now embarked on a new career.

The only thing he knew was farm machinery. It was what he had done since before he had left school. Just by listening to a machine he could diagnose a fault, it really was a unique skill. For years he'd attended, up and down the country, weekly auction sales where he'd noticed there was always a stall on site selling collectable scale models of vintage tractors etc. The old-time farmers cherished these toys in their great hairy hands before handing over large wodges of cash.

Paul's first model was rough, but sold well enough to persuade him to pursue the venture, and by the time he had reached his third he was established. Established and amazed at the double standards of a community who begrudged paying for honest work on real machinery, but would gladly hand over hundreds of pounds for something which amounted to nothing more than a toy!

So the rock had belonged to a farmer who had an affair with my friend's wife. An affair which hit him in the face like a drenching from a pail of cold water, and made him search for and find an inner strength, which he crafted into something quite beautiful.

The community that belittled themselves before him struggle as foot and mouth and subsidy cuts destroy their way of life, and Paul and Jo – well their community has changed too. It may be smaller and more spread out, but real friends, kindred spirits of the same wavelength, are better known in the first few minutes of meeting than some that we call friends will be over the course of a whole lifetime. And best of all, he now has the finances which enable him to do just about whatever he wants, because he makes a fortune from selling dreams of the "good old days" to the retired and redundant of the farming community.

HELEN OF TROY

Philosophical ponderings concerning the who and what we are in relation to the universe tend to be of an extremely personal nature, so when we find someone who thinks like we do, or should I say, has come up with the same thoughts as us, formed from their own pathway through life, there follows a sense of euphoric relief. Firstly, that you're not alone, and secondly that you're not crazy!

When you hear a song, or see a picture that captivates you, even though you haven't the faintest idea of its meaning, you are feeling empathy summoned by the emotions of the artist. Years may go by until you stumble across a phrase or happening which provides the key to the previously enigmatic work. In an instant you understand, you know what the artist meant.

When you make such a connection with a kindred spirit from before our time, then that's even spookier. They leap out of the past to join you in the celebration, and you're smiling, together, united as one.

You would expect the holy books passed down through the ages to be full of such voices, which of course they are, but they don't carry such an impact.

Maybe their words were pertinent at the time of writing but surely, today, isn't it our conscience that tells us that certain moral codes must be observed for our society to work? Things like not stealing, killing or coveting our nei-

☻♂♀

ghbour's wife or husband, you know the sort of thing. Such basic truths call out from our inner self, they might get ignored from time to time, but we no longer require a religious hierarchy to impart the obvious to us.

Of course we recognise and associate with the moral code laid out in religious manuscripts, but any questioning mind will realise that, beyond the obvious, they provide no material or scientific answer to any of the key questions concerning the nature of the universe or man's place in it. They go halfway by confirming our most inner feelings of conscience, but fall short, as if a piece of the story is being withheld.

It's as if an esoteric mystery is purposely perpetuated in order to empower the leaders of such sects.

We've become so used to the boundaries and walls that our culture has built within our heads, that sometimes it's difficult to see beyond them. It's like we're living in a squalid flat with no window, only a door which we've been told we can't open, so we never reach for the handle. When in fact what lies beyond the unlocked door is the most wonderful paradise, where the answer to all the questions we've ever posed are answered.

I'd come up with a theory that explained the workings of the universe. I'd found it by looking beyond the walls created by the holy books.

That being the case, it seemed logical to suppose that the theory may have existed before the establishment of the doctrine laid out in said books.

For this to be so, it would require the existence, before about 2000 years ago, of a philosopher who expounded a scientific theory of a 4th dimension which unites everything in the universe. A philosopher whose theory saw beyond the 3 dimensions with which we define our world. This philosopher was a Roman called Lucretius (99 – 55 BC).

Lucretius followed in a long line of Greek philosophers, called Atomists, coming from as far back as 500 BC.

Leucippus, Democritus, Epicurus and Lucretius; these were the founders of Atomism. A theory that the universe is constructed of particles, their combination giving rise to a unity which explains the nature of things.

They'd worked it out 2500 years ago! They'd come up with a scientific explanation which I'd thought was mine. But they'd had an edge.

Alright, I'd had some help from a history full of scientists, but Lucretius and the boys were closer to 'it all', they were unadulterated. Maybe not pure, but they didn't have mountains of 21st century bull-shit clogging up their senses the way we have.

In the bigger picture they'd just emerged from pre-history. Out of the cradle of civilisation they crawled and staggered, then stepped and danced, their evolving brain and mind urging them to think for themselves - but the archaic bond was strong.

Thousands of years earlier, man's first shot at explaining that bond was to name its different aspects. Zeus the father of gods, Aphrodite goddess of love and fertility, Chaos, Gaia, Eros and Nyx, the Bronze Age Greeks had plenty of gods.

Charting the course of one of these celestial beings as it emerges from pre-history, is worshipped and then deposed, we find, in parallel, the birth of man's ego-conscious, which evolved only to subjugate and denounce those very gods.

From 29000 BC onwards thousand upon thousand of small figures and figurines have been excavated from the pre-historic levels across the Aegean. They are most prolific from Greece and the Eastern Mediterranean from 8000 to 3500 BC.

These small statues became ever more elaborate as time went on, and the vast majority have one thing in common, they celebrate the female form.

It is now widely acknowledged in the archaeological community that these figures celebrated the fecundity, the life-giving force, that flowed from the 'goddess' through the Bronze Age female.

These women had a status that today's women's libbers would die for. Respected as the complete equals of men, they were honoured as the physical incarnation of the Spirit-Goddess of Mother-Earth. In her resided the archetype of beauty, womanhood, sex and fertility and, as the priestess presiding over nature, she would control every aspect of day to day life, having the power to give life, or not, as she chose.

This was a vital, intense time when life was rich, sensuous and short. They embraced it just as it embraced them. Living it to the full, free from all our psychological hang-ups, they just did it.

The population was young and had the cultural energy to match. Women would be mothers by the age of twelve, grandmothers by twenty-four and dead before they were thirty.

This powerful Earth goddess came to be epitomised by Helen of Sparta, better known as Helen of Troy.

Helen is a very important figure. She marks a pivotal time in our evolution. A time when man is testing his developing ego, he is taking his first tentative steps away from the Gods.

In the 10 year Trojan war of 1275 BC the Spartans and Trojans fought over Helen, the physical incarnation of a goddess, perhaps even, "The Goddess". The subsequent accounts of the event, from Homer to Hollywood, are a direct challenge by man as he dares to downgrade the goddess, and all she represents, to the status of whore.

The Trojan Wars mark man's first contest over who would 'own' Helen, the goddess. In doing so, they mark the watershed for mankind, the beginning of the transition from god-centred beings to self-centred beings.

The Roman world of 99 BC, into which Lucretius was born, had broken away from the old gods; the people didn't hear them anymore, it was their own thoughts and wishes that now ruled their heads.

Some, like Lucretius and the others Atomists, were blessed, in that they remained sensitive to the synchronicity they saw and felt in nature, and also possessed the self-control to seek enlightenment in the form of a scientific explanation.

The Roman authorities of the time were struggling to keep order as the populace tested their independence from the gods. Lucretius' philosophy was the last thing they needed.

He hadn't intended it to be anarchistic, but because it stripped away all mystery, showing that all men are equals, it couldn't possibly be 'used' by the state.

No, what the power brokers needed was a religion, a doctrine with which they could control the masses and provide political stability (yet be ambiguous enough to allow the hierarchy freedom to indulge their fancies).

They had a brainwave. They would cobble together a bit of a pick and mix.

They took the passion of a charismatic freedom fighter, a local boy rebelling against a brutal army of occupation, and mixed in Lucretius' theory (having first removed all traces of the scientific explanation of nature's unity) and sold it to the people as 'The Father, Son and Holy Ghost.'

Then, as now, the religion enthusiastically imparted a passionate description of the unity of all things, but gave no answers to the most important questions posed by us humans.

Without Lucretius' scientific explanation, all the major world religions remain vague, lost in a nebulous esoteric mist.

Two thousand years ago the basis for the corruption was understandable. Back then the planet was virginal, there for the taking, but today it's a different matter. Man's insatiable greed and his inability to act as though his physical being is anything other than the centre of the universe, require the devotees of the major world religions to face some cold hard truths.

BEYOND THE WALLS

New York City was the first place where electricity was produced as a commodity, to be sold to the public. The problem the power companies had, was that in those early days electricity was only used for lighting, which meant it was sold to consumers only during the hours of darkness. To increase the sales during the daylight hours, the power companies began producing electrical goods such as cookers, irons and washing machines.

The Americans tend to be at the forefront of such breaking technology – but not so with the mobile telephone.

America was way behind in their changing from the old analogue system to digital, the reason being that the manufacturers wouldn't release the new digital phones until everyone had bought an analogue.

This same milking of outdated technology for the gain of the few can be seen in our continual reliance on fossil fuels. This takes place in the face of desperate warnings from the scientific community, and at a staggering and increasingly obvious cost to the planet's eco-system. Sadly, the politician's interpretation of the 'facts' contributing to the planet's demise tend to contradict those of the scientist's. Such uncertainty over the 'facts' makes it easy for one to sit on the fence. After all, even if our culture is to blame for the mismanagement of global resources, things don't seem too bad to us citizens of Good Old

●♂Ψ

Blighty. The nasty side, the end result happens a long way from home. We're looked after, if you know what I mean, our apathy and silence bought. Let's face it, being poor in this country has no real comparison to being poor in say Somalia, Colombia, Nigeria, Iraq, Haiti, Paraguay, Ghana, the Philippines; the list just goes on and on. The simple fact is that we, the minority in the world, oppress the majority. Not wishing to rock the boat, we keep our heads down, but in these days of instant access to information on the internet super-highway, it becomes increasingly difficult to deny who we really are. We are an obvious link in the chain of unfair trade and unjust debt; we seek absolution from our guilty conscience through charity donations that only serve to compound the tragedy. The imploring eyes of the starving beg not for our aid, but for us to be honest with ourselves.

Our culture is, to all intents and purposes, the world government; we put it into power as a democratic dictatorship.

We don't have to look beyond the walls of our own culture to see the out-dated, vested interests of those in power being sold to the masses; putting profit and gain for the few before common sense and the well-being of the many. The struggles that our culture embraces to secure our supply of oil is frightening. It's price is so high that 'green' fuels, such as vegetable oil and hydrogen, keep popping into the news; and what of the massive potential for energy drawn from the tides that surround our island. Why do you think it is that rather than actively promoting such eco-friendly alternatives the government merely gives them lip-service?

The biggest offenders in this gallery of the ridiculous are the religions of the world. With their books of moral codes they would deceive us into believing we could not reach those conclusions ourselves. The initial conspiracy to conceal a simple truth, and the following complicity that allowed that knowledge to become lost for 2000 years, has brought the planet to the very edge of the abyss. The only way back from that edge is for us to open our eyes to the big picture. Think outside the box.

In December 2003 a strong northerly sank our boat *Eos* at her jetty – twice. The jetty had been falling to pieces for years, and I'm certain that a combination of the gales and my rough repairs led to the catastrophes. The first time she sank I managed to get her up off the bottom on my own. With my hands numbed in the cold water I was almost in tears when I finally finished bailing her out. The job didn't end there. Because the engine had submerged, it had to be removed from the boat and the salt water cleaned from the carburettor and fuel tank. That wasn't so difficult, and was done at *Broadview* with it clamped to the garden fence. As these engines are water-cooled you can't run them for more than a couple of seconds on a garden fence, or indeed anywhere out of water, without them seizing. With this in mind, as soon as it fired I shut it off and took it down to the now floating *Eos*. It was a glorious day. Not a breath of wind, a clear blue sky and the tide was coming in, so I thought I'd take a ride down the channel in order to clear out the engine and maybe come across *Eos's* oars which had gone missing in the capsizing. The day was perfect.

The afternoon light gave the deep green mosses along the bank the texture of finest velvet, and the reeds, now fawn and dry, arched their heads heavy with seed across the river, forming a tunnel through which we slowly emerged into the ever-widening expanse of the estuary. I was the only person out. The stillness of this place was eerie, the noise of the outboard an intrusion, and so, putting my faith in my repair, I shut it off and just drifted for a while. It was awe-inspiring. One of those occasions where the blue of the sky and water meet and become one. Such massive expanses of nature swallow you up, humbling you in the process. And there I sat for several minutes, deep in meditation, immersed in the beauty of my surroundings.

I had completely chilled out when the weirdest thing happened, which sent me sprawling backwards off the seat, floundering in the bottom of the boat. Right next to *Eos,* so close I could see his eyeball, a massive bull seal jumped out of the water, his flipper almost touching the side. *Eos* lurched about amongst the ripples of which we were the epicentre and, although the peace had been disturbed, there was still the feeling that I was completely alone – except that now the feeling had changed from serenity to fear.

Now, ridiculous as it might seem, I thought, what if this 30 stones of blubber decides to jump into the boat? In a state of panic I snapped into the routine of starting the engine. It didn't fire first pull. O God, I'm going to die! Savaged by a seal. Second pull it spluttered and picked up, and with my serene thoughts in tatters, I hydroplaned back into the channel as fast as my fifteen horses would take me. The up side was that, on the way back, I found both our lost oars. With all things considered, it had been one of the most exciting outings I had had for a long while.

The plan had been to take *Eos* out over the rest of the winter and rebuild the jetty but, loth to deprive myself of the possibility of such wonderful adventures, I made a few alterations to her mooring ropes and decided to leave her in. Big mistake.

That night as I lay in bed, I could hear the northerly gale pounding on the tiles above me, and at first light I went down to the quay. I could have wept. *Eos* was on the bottom again! This time I couldn't get it up without the help of Ray and his father, Ray senior, a sailor who had survived the Russian convoys of World War Two, and who now in his 90s shouted encouragement from the slipway. This time we took *Eos* and the engine straight out, and a month or so later rebuilt the jetty. All the same, I don't leave her in over winter anymore.

Not so with Johnny Picnic, the owner of the deli (*Picnic Fayre)* in Cley. He has a jetty just down from ours where he keeps a boat, which he shares with a friend.

In January 2005 after a night of winds of a ferocity to parallel the ones that sank *Eos,* I had a phone call from Picnic asking if I'd give him a hand to raise his boat from the bottom.

I first got to know Picnic about ten years ago when we were looking for a drummer for our band, *The Point.* We'd auditioned several hopefuls, and none seemed to fit the bill until Picnic, who lived just a couple of hundred yards away with his wife and two young sons, pedalled down the track in his dinner hour and asked if he could have a go.

Picnic and his wife had founded the deli in 1984. Previously a blacksmith's shop, which, rumour had it, made cannon for the fighting of the Armada, it had in more recent times been a gift shop where Mother had worked for a while. She is the proud owner of a paper knife, which was one of the last items a visiting black-smith had crafted in the forge. Over the years Picnic made his business a great success, he put his heart into it, although, sadly, his marriage came to an end. That was a gloomy time for the usually effervescent Picnic, but just when his darkest hour was upon him, an enchan-ting breeze blew into his life. Her name was Victoria – and Picnic breathed, and laughed, and lived again. In the fullness of time they wed, and ever since Picnic has glo-wed with such contentment that at times I fear my friend will surely burst.

With the deli doing well, Picnic found himself in the com-fortable position of being able to employ a chap called Lawrence as a manager, which afforded him the free time he needed to control his ever expanding business.

Across the road from the deli is the old butcher's shop, now a book shop and art gallery owned by Michael Chapman, the owner of the other half of Picnic's boat.

Picnic had rallied the troops to help with the raising. He had asked Ray, Lawrence and Michael Chapman to come along to lend a hand. Now I considered that Ray with his knowledge of boats was essential to such an operation, but never having made the acquaintance of Picnic's other two friends, I couldn't imagine what sort of input they would be capable of.

At 8 am we all met at the quay, where Lawrence and Chapman mostly watched as John, Ray and I righted and then raised the boat. Their not taking part didn't matter in the slightest, we were too many as it was for the job in hand, but what I did find interesting was seeing them interact with John, who was also interacting with Ray and me. I began to notice how we had split into two groups, and, unless I am much mistaken, it was the background of our schooling that separated us.

My secondary modern education had an old boys' club just like that of the public school system. Each seems to bond ex-pupils in a shared understanding along with its unspoken rules and rituals, designed to protect and separate its members from "the others."

I used to let class issues get to me, and it's only recently that I've managed to see why. It's the upper class that to a greater extent runs the country and in turn the planet. It's easy to be tricked into believing that this class would do so from a moral higher ground, that they would wield the power invested in them in the best interests of the whole planet. The imbalance we see today in our ecosystem and in the distribution of wealth around the planet, stems directly from the moral weaknesses of what I once perceived to be the upper class. In short the people who are running the show aren't running things for everybody, but just to make sure that they remain 'first at the trough'.

Twenty years ago there were promises by western governments that the unfair trade restrictions would be dealt with. Twenty years ago the warning over the greenhouse effect had become a plea. We were told that if we didn't make a move to eco-friendly methods of energy production we would destroy our ecosystem.

Little was done, and the consequence is that twenty years later the planet is on the brink of melt down, and unfair trade restrictions still hold the people of those oppressed countries in a position of disadvantage. The warnings over our choice of energy production were ignored, taking us into a time frame where we're told it is too late to make that change. Scientists calculate that within perhaps as little as fifteen years the damage caused to our eco-system by the continued use of fossil fuels will be irreversible. There is no longer time to phase in alternative sources of energy production.

You can't help laugh at the irony as nuclear power is now being promoted as a short term measure, in order to buy us the time we need to make the transition to safe, renewable, eco-friendly power production.

And as the time clock ticks away, we make pathetically inadequate excuses and long overdue gestures of sympathy. Yes, we cut some of the debt, but in real terms there is actually a drop in aid and still no fair trade. We continue to watch from our cosy little world as the horrors unfold. Tick-tock-tick-tock – we're sitting on a time bomb!

John Ratcliffe
(12-12-1896 to 22-03-1959)

I've always been proud of being a Balding. Proud of the fact that my family has lived in this area for centuries, but always in the back of my mind there is the reminder of an old black and white photo I have of my mother when she was a teenager. The resemblance between us when we were each passing through those teenage years is startling. That being the case, it seems obvious that there is a great deal of Mother's side of the family in me. Her father, my grandfather, had died at the age of 63 when I was only 3, so sadly I have no memory of him. I knew his life had been eventful, but I'd never taken the time to piece together all the snippets of stories which Mother had told me over the years. When I did so, it revealed a life not occupied by fanciful dreams but a life of actually having a go, lived to the full despite persistent visitations of misfortune and adversity.

Born in Greater Manchester, John, who was always referred to as Jack, enlisted to fight in the First World War at the age of 17. Two years later, in 1916, during one of the great pushes, he was shot through the ankle and invalided out. Upon his return to England he met and married my grandmother, Julia Wordingham, a Cley girl who was working in Manchester at the time. That was in 1917. They had two children, my mother, Joan, and John.

He then went to work in a foundry that made railway engines. Jack was 26 when an accident at this work took out his eye, for which he received £375 compensation.

With his compensation Jack and Julia moved to Cley, where they toyed with keeping chickens, but in 1926 they gave it up, deciding to seek their fortune in London as proprietors of a guest house. The house, called *Richmond Terrace,* cost £900, and they ran it until 1941 – when the Germans bombed it.

After the war the house was repaired and sold and, once again my grandparents returned to the North Norfolk coast, where they became the licensees of the *Anchor* public house, which used to be at the bottom of Blakeney High Street. Here he had to console his daughter as she mourned the death of her reckless husband in his misjudged Spitfire fly-by.

In 1953 they bought the properties known as *The Willows* in Wiveton, which were wrecked during a storm on the very day he made the purchase, drowning the sitting tenant. After making the repairs to *The Willows* they moved in, only for Jack to die three years later of an aneurysm.

Jack achieved so much in the face of such incredible bad luck that I cant help admire the man, and it really puts into perspective how little I have actually achieved. Perhaps this might sound ungrateful, but to find myself at 49 running our business here at *Broadview* it all seems to be a bit of a dead end. Especially with all these thoughts concerning the bigger picture running through my head. Mid-life crisis? Well maybe, but I can't help thinking that Jack wouldn't have just sat it out, waiting for the time bomb to explode!

I must be about 10 years younger than Trevor. We grew up in neighbouring villages, went to the same schools, used the same local. It was a tight community.

The White Horse at Blakeney and to a lesser extent *The George* at Cley were, during the 70's, the meeting places for North Norfolk s punk chapter. Oh dear – we were so ridiculous!

The introversions that my personality had adopted always kept me at the edge of that outburst of self-expression. Looking back, maybe that was fortunate, at the time it didn't seem so; I desperately wanted to join in.

Condemned to watching from the sidelines, one of the few people I found for company was Trevor.

Trevor was born into a travellers' family who had chosen to settle in Cley.

He'd got into a bit of trouble in his teens, nothing serious, but the following incident, although it seemed trivial at the time, would change the direction of his life forever.

It all started about 3 miles away at a local dump. The Billsa Pit was vast, covering many acres. It had originally been the quarry that provided the aggregate for a nearby airfield built during the Second World War.

In my youth such places were our playgrounds, the Billsa being the strangest and scariest of them all, where anything, and I'm certain *everything*, had been dumped. It was that sort of place.

Whilst ferreting around at this dump, Trevor came across, believe it or not, an old, broken, bren gun! Which was quite a find for a teenager.

He took it home and adapted it to fire some rounds of live ammunition, which he'd managed to scrounge from a friend whose father wouldn't miss them. He told another friend about the gun, and this boy's moral concerns over the dangers posed by such a lethal weapon prompted him to share his worries with a father figure of the community, a Mr Billy Bishop, the famous warden of the Cley nature reserve. The warden felt he had no other choice than to have a word with the village constable, who paid Trevor a visit. With 'the frighteners' put on him, Trevor was given the option of joining the army or being arrested, he chose the former and went off to Aden, to see the world and fight in a war which he didn't understand and should never have been a part of.

When his time was up, having seen several of his friends killed in action, Trevor returned to Cley but found it increasingly difficult to fit into the material-driven culture. Alcohol and drugs became the place from where he chose to watch that world, and during the 1970s that was the place I also felt most at ease – and so for a while we sat together. Time moves everything on in this dimension, and while I hate to use the phrase "buckle down" I guess that's what I did. While I tried to keep my concessions to the Thatcherite values of the time to a bare minimum. Trevor had no inclination to. He just couldn't see the sense in it. He wanted no part of it and his only escape was to anaesthetise himself until everything that conformed to the values he loathed no longer impinged on his world.

Unfortunately, some of those objects which demanded conformity also fell into the in-between ground of things he loved. His wife and children and then his home. They all drifted away from him.

Trevor returned to his elderly parents and lovingly cared for them until they passed away – leaving him alone.

Alone, that is, except for his friend and drinking partner Barry, another soul who refused to take part in our senseless game.

After his mother and father had passed on, Trevor was allowed to live in their council house, which was an unusual place. His parents had been the last generation of a gypsy family who had come to rest in Cley. The rich culture they'd left behind was reflected in the house's decoration. Traditional paintings of flowers and vines issued from ceiling centres, spiralling away out and down the walls and up the stair well.

Trevor's father had created a large collection of carved and painted walking sticks, each one skilfully adorned with animals and flowers, which were kept in a bundle in the corner of the lounge. Fearful of said sticks disappearing whilst "out of it," Trevor made a decision which might seem strange to those of us rooted in a world of material possessions. He visited his friends – and gave these wonderful works of art away. This was typical of Trevor's way of thinking.

After his parents had settled, his father practised the trade of mole catcher. An art requiring such an affinity between hunter and quarry it has to be witnessed to be believed.

The skill was passed to Trevor, who one day while mole catching in Cley found a coin that had been unearthed by one of the furry little creatures. Upon further investigation the coin turned out to be a medallion issued in Porto Bello, Panama, in 1739, to commemorate its capture by an admiral of the British Fleet.

Porto Bello is a natural deep-water harbour, which had been used for centuries by the Spanish for the removal of plundered Inca and Aztec gold, making it quite a trophy for the British.

The port first came to my notice through my interest in a German explorer, Alexander Humboldt, who had between 1799 and 1804 explored the tropical South Americas. Why the interest in Humboldt?

Humboldt saw the interaction of nature as a whole and sought to understand that unity. His uncompromising work in the fields of climatology, geology, mineralogy, terrestrial magnetism, botany, zoology, political economy and ethnography was the stimulus that motivated Charles Darwin. The rest is history.

Fascinated by this medallion, I asked Trevor that if he ever had cause to sell it, would he give me first refusal. At the time he declined, only to approach me at the village shop a couple of weeks later and give it to me. He would accept nothing for it.

On a cold February afternoon in 2004, after a particular heavy binge, Trevor said goodbye to his friend Barry and watched him wobble off on his bicycle for the mile journey to his home in Blakeney. Mid-way, at the foot of the steep hill just below *Broadview,* Barry fell off into a drainage ditch. Although the ditch had but a few feet of water in it – he drowned.

I wondered if his friend's demise might bring home the precariousness of Trevor's chosen path, but you know how it goes, - old dogs and new tricks.

Trevor comes round from time to time, when we have a mole problem. We talk about old times and the ways of mutual acquaintances. His course is set to a way of life which ironically is in itself a work of art, a public statement that says "I don't want to take part in your ridiculously destructive culture"!

At least Trevor is making a protest, as did Barry – the ultimate protest. For all my strong words and big ideas, what had been mine? What had I actually done over the past 49 years? I would like to think my craving for material possessions have been kept to a minimum. I have built my own home, but lots of people do that. There has been the occasional outburst of half-hearted whingeing, but other than that, looking at the bigger picture there hasn't been much evidence of any sort of radical protest amongst it at all! I have simply watched as the planet approached melt down. In my defence I might argue that such awful acts of ecological mis-management have never happened before. Not with this intensity, not with this degree of finality. I knew no different. I'd been brought up in a culture that had a fundamental flaw and, along with everybody else, I'd turned an apathetic blind eye.

After Jack Ratcliffe lost his eye in the foundry accident he and Julia moved from Manchester to Cley. This was around 1929, the time of the great depression. Things were pretty bad up north, so Jack's father and mother, and the remainder of his brothers and sisters who didn't have any work, came down and joined them. Despite being in his 70s and having only one lung, Jack's father, along with the rest of the family, walked all the way.

All the people who've made my world have touched me, some more than others. I felt the least I could do was to write their stories down. So that's what I've done.

THE DISCLAIMER

A Scottish guest analogised that a plane flying from London to New York on auto pilot is 90% of the time on the wrong course. It drifts away from its true heading until the limit of error is sensed and the automatic controls bring the plane back to its flight path but it soon wanders away again and so the process continues.

Life, he concluded, is just like that.

SPECIAL THANKS

There's been a whole host of angels who, masquerading as people, have helped make my dream a reality, the list would fill many pages but I couldn't go without saying a special thak you to

Connie Crescenzi and everyone at Arti Grafiche

Ray Medler

John Sykes

Ray Millard
&
Russell Brown